CLEVER CARD TRICKS

FOR THE HOPELESSLY CLUMSY

CLEVER CARD TRICKS
FOR THE HOPELESSLY CLUMSY

BY BOB LONGE

BARNES
& NOBLE
BOOKS
NEW YORK

Library of Congress Cataloging-in-Publication Data Available

2 4 6 8 10 9 7 5 3 1

Published by Sterling Publishing Co., Inc.
387 Park Avenue South, New York, NY 10016

© 2005 by Sterling Publishing Co., Inc.

Designed by StarGraphics Studio

This book is composed of material from the following Sterling titles:
Clever Card Tricks for the Hopelessly Clumsy © 2001 by Bob Longe
Easy Card Tricks © 1995 by Bob Longe
Mystifying Card Tricks © 1997 by Bob Longe

ISBN 0-7607-6781-5

TABLE OF CONTENTS

TRICKS (CONTINUED)

INTRODUCTION

An argument can be made that almost every calling requires some amount of selling. It's certainly true of such diverse occupations as teaching, medicine, journalism, and law. And it's especially true of the performance of magic. The tricks are your product; the performance is selling.

A sales representative doesn't simply run the vacuum cleaner and expect a sale; he explains the benefits, indicates how much easier life will be, and paints a picture of total cleanliness accomplished with ease. And with magic, you don't just perform a trick and hope for the best: You must sell the trick. Some magicians, particularly stage performers, accomplish this with props, music, costumes, and such. Even so, in most instances the principal selling tool is the voice.

This is certainly true of card tricks. Apart from the deck itself, what other tools do you have? So you should use your voice cleverly and thoughtfully. What are you trying to sell? Yourself, of course. The group should feel that you're a good person. If you are, this should be an easy sell. So let's not worry about that. Basically, then, you're trying to sell the spectators on the validity of the trick you're doing. In other words, you're trying to fool them. And, at the same time, you want to entertain them. Your patter, your demeanor, your entire presentation should be aimed at this dual goal.

So try to develop patter for each trick. Give it a lot of thought. Present a story that's either serious or amusing, but is always interesting. Perhaps include an anecdote or two. (If you tell a joke and people laugh, that's a joke. If you tell a joke and nobody laughs, that's an illustrative anecdote.) You can orally create an atmosphere of mystery, recount a tale that will misdirect the attention of the group, or make a series of silly remarks that evoke laughter. The possibilities are endless.

As you practice a trick, be sure to include the patter. Thus your patter will improve as you perfect the mechanics, and you'll end up with a perfectly integrated and entertaining trick.

In this book you'll find a fascinating collection of card tricks that especially lend themselves to patter, for you're involved in all sorts of mental magic: prediction, strange coincidence, telepathy, feats of the conscious mind, and a number of hilarious mental tricks. Patter themes should readily spring to mind. If they don't, however, I offer patter suggestions for almost every trick.

When you decide to do mental magic with cards, you must decide whether you're going to be serious about it or not. Are you going to purport that you have superior mental powers? I prefer to be just as baffled as the rest of the group, taking the attitude, "I don't know why it works; it just does." I figure that I'm just doing card tricks; why would I want to pretend that I have some sort of mysterious access to the ultimate powers of the universe?

A deck of cards is ideal for performing mental magic because so much variety is possible. In fact, using some of the tricks presented here, you can do an entire show of mental magic. Or—my preference—you can include several as a part of your regular program.

If you prefer not to do mental magic, you may perform many of these items as simply mystifying card tricks. The only difference is the patter.

I'm very proud of this collection, and I'm sure you'll find many tricks that you'll enjoy performing.

Moves and Maneuvers

Preposterous Patter

Here we have some patter lines that many find funny. Some are original, but most have been concocted by others, and are quite ancient. Obviously, a joke isn't old to someone who hasn't heard it before, so you may find some of these useful.

But that is not my main purpose in presenting them to you. I hope that you'll observe the sort of lines that have found success. As with all humor, you'll find here the unexpected, the well-turned phrase, or the just-plain-silly. Perhaps some of these will give you some ideas on how to develop lines of your own to use with your tricks. In all of the tricks presented here, you will find patter suggestions that may inspire you to devise original comical lines to enhance your performance.

On the other hand, depending on your nature, you may decide to make a more serious presentation. Regardless, here are the lines, most of which are very familiar to experienced magicians.

1) "Would you like to see a card trick? All right, then I'll have to get out my trick cards. I'm kidding. This is an ordinary deck of marked cards. Yes, they're marked. See the marks? This is a queen of spades. This is a 7 of hearts. This is a 5 of clubs. They're all marked."

2) "Take a card, any card …" The spectator does; "… except that one."

3) "We have here an ordinary deck of 57 cards."

4) Point up one sleeve. "Nothing here." Point up the other sleeve. "Nothing here." Point to your head. "And very little here."

5) "I believe your card is a cherry-colored card."
"No, it isn't."
"You've never heard of black cherries?"

6) "Your card is a licorice-colored card."

"No, it isn't."

"You've never heard of red licorice?"

7) "Do you know one card from the other?"

"Sure."

"Okay. Name one card. Come on … you can do it."

"6 of spades."

"Excellent. Now for something really tough. What's the other?"

"Jack of spades."

"Right! You *do* know one card from the other. Terrific job!"

8) "I am the most amazed person when one of my experiments happens to work. The magical result just astonishes me. When I do this stunt, however, I seldom have to worry about that."

9) With the right spectator, you might even be moderately insulting: "Hold out your hand, please… No, the clean one. Just kidding. Heck, my hands are almost as dirty as yours."

10) "Take a card. Now show it to your friends. This shouldn't take long."

11) "This is the first time I've ever made that mistake… again."

12) "I can't believe it! This entire deck of cards is printed upside down. Of course it's kind of hard to tell."

Control

Every magician who does card tricks must have some way of controlling a card after it has been chosen. Most methods require considerable skill. Here's one that's very easy.

Simplicity Itself

In some instances, this control works best. For example, you might want to bring the chosen card to a fairly high number from the top. This would do perfectly, as I'll explain.

Before the spectator chooses a card, sneak a peek at the bottom card of the deck. You can do this as you separate the deck in two, preparing to do a riffle shuffle (Illus. 1). Then, when you shuffle, keep the card on the bottom. Easier yet, look at the bottom card as you tap the side of the deck on the table, apparently evening up the cards (Illus. 2). More suggestions for peeking at the bottom card can be found near the beginning of the tricks "The Way Back," on page 27, and "Piles of Magic," on page 66.

So you know the bottom card of the deck. Fan out the deck, and a spectator selects a card. Close up the deck. From the top of the deck, lift off a small packet and drop it onto the table. Lift off

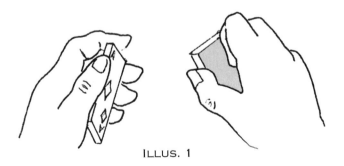

ILLUS. 1

ILLUS. 2

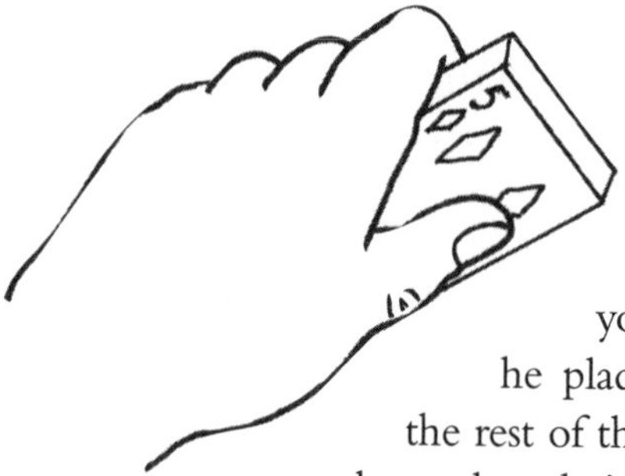

another small packet and drop it on top of the first one. After dropping several packets like this, say to the spectator, "Put your card here whenever you want." After you drop one of your packets, he places his card on top. You put the rest of the deck on top of it. Even up the cards and pick them up. The card that you peeked at is now above the chosen card.

Start fanning through the cards, their faces toward yourself. Mutter something about, "This is going to be really hard." Fan off several cards. Cut them to the rear of the deck. Fan off several more. Again, cut them to the rear. You're establishing a pattern so that it won't seem so odd when you finally cut the chosen card to a key position.

Let's say you simply want the card available on top of the deck. Continue fanning groups of cards and placing them at the rear until you see that you'll soon arrive at the key card. The card on the near side of the key card is the one chosen by the spectator (Illus. 3). Cut the cards so that the key card becomes

ILLUS. 3

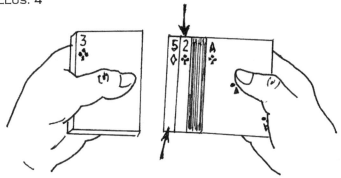

the top card of the deck (Illus. 4). Just below it, of course, is the chosen card. Turn the deck face down.

"I can't seem to find your card." Turn over the top card of the deck (the key card). "This isn't it, is it?" No. Turn the card over and stick it into the middle of the deck. Turn the deck face up. "How about this one?" No. Take the bottom card and stick it into the middle of the deck. Turn the deck face down. The chosen card is at your disposal on top of the deck.

Suppose, for purposes of a specific trick, you want the chosen card to be tenth from the top. Again you start by fanning off small groups and cutting them to the rear of the deck. When you get to the chosen card, you start counting to yourself. You count the chosen card as "One." Count the next card as "Two." Cut the cards so that the card at "Ten" becomes the top card. The chosen card is now tenth from the top.

FALSE CUTS

An efficient false cut should be done casually, just as a genuine cut would be performed. Often magicians manipulate the cards back and forth between their hands, rapidly shift piles here and there, and finally end up with a single pile. Naturally, spectators don't know exactly what happened, but they sure as heck know that *something phony was done.* This is not always bad; sometimes it's alright to show that you're skillful. But many of us prefer to keep our skills—however minimal—secret. I recommend this.

JUST A CASUAL CUT

Hold the deck in your left hand. With your right hand, lift off the top portion of the deck and place it face down onto the table. Make some casual remark. At the same time, *without looking* at the card, take the rest of the deck with your right hand. Place this pile *to the right* of those on the table.

Continue commenting. Glance down at the cards on the table. Pick up the pile on the right and place it on top of those on the left. Pick up the combined pile.

The cards retain their original order.

AND ANOTHER

With the left hand, take the bottom portion of the deck. The left hand should be palm down, and the packet should be grasped with the second finger at the far end, the first finger on top, and the thumb at the near end. The top portion of the deck is retained in your right hand (Illus. 5). Gesture with the left hand as you make a comment. At the same time, drop your right hand somewhat, so that it becomes lower than the left hand.

Place the left-hand portion onto the table. Put the right-hand portion on top of it (Illus. 6). Pick up the entire deck with the right hand.

The cards are back in order.

ILLUS. 5

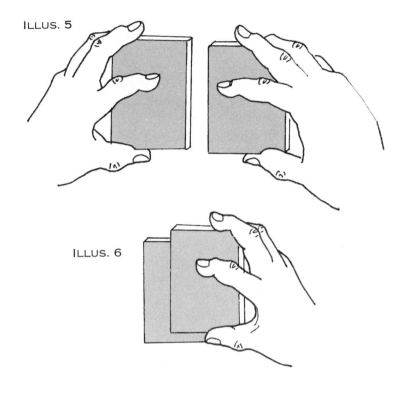

ILLUS. 6

ROLL-UP CUT

I designed this cut specifically for the gambling trick "Really Wild," which appears in my book *World's Greatest Card Tricks.* There is no sleight of hand, and the deck is kept in order.

Since the cut does not appear ordinary, it can work well if you just give it a fancy name. For instance, you might say, "I'll just give the cards my 'inside-outside over-and-out cut.'" Or, "Here's my famous 'whoop-dee-doo and row-dee-dow cut.'" Actually, you can give it any extravagant name; I generally call it something different every time.

Hold the deck in the dealing position in your left hand. With your left thumb, flip the deck face up. (For an example of this move, see Illus. 15, page 28.) If the move is too difficult, simply grip the ends of the deck between the right fingers and thumb, and turn it over (Illus. 7).

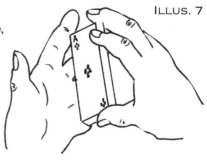

With your right thumb, grip about a quarter of the face-up deck on the left side (Illus. 8). Lift this packet, pivoting it to the right, as though opening a book from the back (Illus. 9). Let the packet fall face down onto your right hand. Place it face down to your left.

Flip the rest of the deck over with your left thumb so that the cards are now face down. As before, if this is too difficult, just turn the cards face down with your right hand.

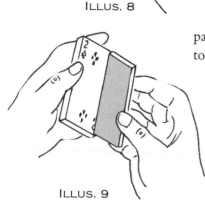

ILLUS. 8

With your right thumb, lift about a third of the face-down cards on the left side. Pivot these over, as before (as though opening a book from the back). Let the packet fall face up onto your right hand. Set the packet onto the table a few inches to the right of the first packet.

Again, flip the rest of the deck over with your left thumb, or turn it face up with your right hand. With your right thumb, pivot off about half of the cards and set them face down on the table to the right of the other two packets.

ILLUS. 9

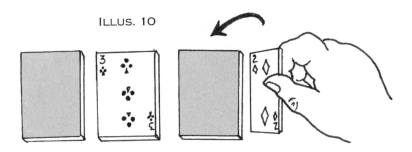

Remaining in your left hand is a packet of face-up cards. Take the packet into your right hand and set it face up to the right of the others. Pause, saying, "Now comes the hard part."

With your right hand, grasp the right side of the packet you just placed down. Turn this packet over on top of the packet to its left, as though closing the back portion of a book (Illus. 10). In the same way, turn the combined packet over and place it on the packet to its left. Once more, turn the combined packet over and place it on the packet to its left—the first packet you placed down.

Even up the cards. The deck is face down and in the precise order it was at the beginning.

If you follow the instruction with a deck of cards, it will seem that the cards can't possibly be in their original order. It just doesn't seem logical. Maybe I should have called it the "illogical cut."

Note

When lifting off the packets to place them onto the table, you may prefer to grasp them at the ends with the palm down right hand, fingers at the outer end and thumb at the inner end. As with the other method, you pivot the packet in an arc to the right, as though opening a book from the back. Then place the packet onto the table.

MILKING THE CARDS

This is actually a fairly simple procedure with a small packet of cards. The idea is to slide off the top and bottom cards together and place the two together onto the table. Again, you slide off the top and bottom cards together and place these two on top of the first two. You continue like this until the pile is exhausted. The move is important in quite a few tricks.

ILLUS. 11

Let's get more specific. Hold a packet of cards from above in your palm-down left hand, thumb at the inner end, first finger resting loosely on top, and the other fingers at the outer end (Illus. 11). Your palm-up right hand lightly grips the top and bottom cards, thumb on top and fingers on the bottom. The right hand pulls the top and bottom cards to the right until they clear the packet (Illus. 12).

The two cards are set onto the table. Draw off two more cards, dropping them on top of the first two. Continue until all the cards are in a pile on the table.

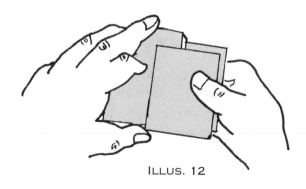

ILLUS. 12

THE UP-AND-DOWN SHUFFLE

Anytime you perform this maneuver, you refer to it as a shuffle. Actually, it is not. It's a subtle method of rearranging the cards to your advantage. Usually, it is performed with a packet of cards—somewhere between ten and 25.

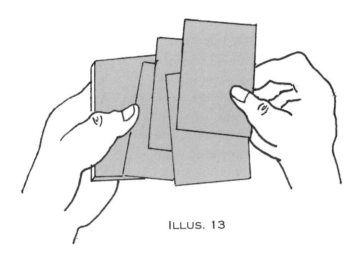

ILLUS. 13

Start by holding the packet in the left hand in the dealing position. Push off the top card with your left thumb and take it with your right hand. Push off the next card with your left thumb. Move your right hand forward (away from you) a bit. Take this second card below the first card in your right hand. This second card should be two inches or so below the first card.

Move the cards in your right hand back toward you. Push off a third card with your left thumb. Take it below the first two cards so that it is even with the first card you drew off.

Move the cards in your right hand back toward you. Push off a fourth card with your left thumb. This card goes on top of the others and is even with the second card you drew off (Illus. 13).

Continue alternating like this until the packet is exhausted.

Hold the upper group with your left hand as, with your right hand, you strip out the lower group from the others (Illus. 14). This group goes on top of the cards remaining in your left hand.

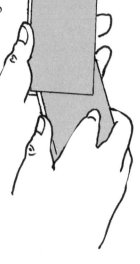

ILLUS. 14

Notes

1) Depending on the trick, in the first move of the shuffle you may move the top card *down* or toward you, the next card up, the next card down, and so forth.

2) Depending on the trick, when you strip out the lower group (the cards nearest you), these will sometimes go *below* the cards you hold in your left hand.

3) Speed is not needed for this maneuver. If you take your time, you can do it quite easily.

WHAT IF THINGS GO WRONG?

You have the wrong card! For some inexplicable reason, the trick simply didn't work.

There are two cardinal rules: (1) Under no conditions try the trick again. (2) Don't blame the spectators.

You failed; accept it. Why did you fail? The possibilities are unlimited. Try one of these excuses, for instance:

"Just what I thought, the deck was too slippery."

"Well, the score is now one to nothing, your favor."

"What was your card?" She names it. "Just as I suspected. That's my 'bad luck' card."

"I'm not surprised. That trick never works. Let's try one that does."

"You have to admit one thing: If that worked, it would have been one heck of a great trick."

"It's my fault, really. I washed my hands this morning and now I can't do a thing with them."

"Gee! And only a few minutes ago, that used to be my favorite card trick."

I'm sure you can think of dozens of other silly excuses. The point is: Say something somewhat amusing and then get on with it; show another trick—preferably one that you're sure will work. Most will forget that you ever goofed up. And many will think it's all part of the show.

Above all, don't let it bother you. Remain composed as you proceed with your tricks. The old show-biz saying applies here: "Don't let them see you sweat."

One-Two-Three Shift

Years ago, I devised a sort of false shuffle that can be used with a relatively small packet of cards. It's actually a mixing procedure that brings a particular card to a desired position in the packet. Several tricks in the book call for this maneuver.

Suppose you want to pretend to mix a packet of 12 cards but actually keep it in the same order. You'd transfer 12 cards from the top to the bottom of the packet, moving one, two, or three cards at a time. As you transfer the cards, you, of course, keep a silent count. The specific number that you move each time is irrelevant so long as the total number transferred is correct. Let's do it together.

You're holding a packet of 12 cards. Fan off two cards from the top of the packet, take them into the right hand, and place them on the bottom of the packet. Say to yourself, "Two."

Move one card from the top to the bottom, mentally saying, "Three" (2 + 1 = 3).

Fan out three cards from the top. Take them into the right hand and place them on the bottom. Say to yourself, "Six" (3 + 3 = 6).

Spread out two cards from the top, take them into the right hand, and place them on the bottom. Say to yourself, "Eight" (6 + 2 = 8).

Move one card from the top to the bottom, mentally saying, "Nine" (8 + 1 = 9).

Fan out three cards from the top and put them on the bottom, saying to yourself, "12" (9 + 3 = 12).

All done. And the packet is in the same order as when you began.

Let's try another example. Suppose you have a packet of 20 cards and you wish to bring the bottom card to the ninth position from the top. Simply subtract 9 from 20, giving you 11. Now transfer 11 cards from the top to the bottom of the packet, moving one, two, or three cards at a time. As above, keep a silent count.

You must try to make it look as though you're not counting, that you're merely mixing the cards, and that the number you move each time is irrelevant, as is the total number you move. It helps if you perform the entire "shuffle" as sloppily as you can.

DEVELOPING A ROUTINE

Several excellent routines can be built around the tricks in this book. How many tricks to use in a routine? There's no right answer. You should be ready to perform as many as seven or eight tricks, but when interest wanes, immediately go to your climactic blockbuster.

You might finish eight tricks and your audience clamors for more. Usually, I'll perform a few more tricks. The important thing is to quit on a high note. Don't wait until your audience drifts. Don't let yourself get carried away with your performance. Some magicians, when the audience grows apathetic, will say something like, "Here! Let me show you this one." You want to be admired, not pitied. It's better to stop a trick or two short than to show even one trick too many.

It's also true that some groups will want to see every trick you can show them. In this case, I'd recommend that you do your first routine, and follow it with a shorter routine that also has a strong closing trick. Then quit. Save a little something for next time.

How to develop a routine? For the most part, it's a matter of trial and error, but there are a few fundamentals. The first trick should be an attention-getter, and it shouldn't be lengthy. The last trick should be one of your best, leaving a strong favorable impression. In between, you should have considerable variety.

You have at least three possible themes for your routine:

1) Do an entire "mental" routine. Sufficient variety is provided as you read minds, predict the future, and perform other psychic feats. You are *not* doing card tricks; you are demonstrating peculiar phenomena.

2) Choose tricks that are strong on audience participation. "The more the merrier" definitely applies here.

3) Perform a number of different types of card trick. I choose some tricks with strong audience participation, and I might pick out a mental trick or two. Emphasize diversity.

An excellent opening trick would be "Easy Opener," on page 157. The trick is arresting and it has strong spectator involvement. Another good opener would be "Count Off," on page 112. You might choose an opener in which some of the cards are prearranged. "Cutting the Aces," on page 165 is a quick, startling miracle, and "Most Magicians," on page 163 is a snappy routine in itself.

Eventually, you'll find an opening trick you really like and that works well for you.

To fill out your routine, choose a trick or two from each of the various chapters.

HIDE & SEEK. In this section, you'll find a number of "discovery" tricks. I particularly enjoy "Poker Location," on page 117 and "Computer Whiz," on page 121, but try them all.

MAGIC SPELLS. A spelling trick always goes over well, and here you will find four of them. My favorite is "Number, Please," on page 140.

UNEXPECTED REVERSALS. Audiences love a trick in which a chosen card mysteriously turns face up. Particularly clever is "Fan Out," on page 145.

RED & BLACK MAGIC. These tricks involve red and black cards. All three are clever and effective.

LONG-DISTANCE CALLS. Here are three captivating tricks in which the telephone is used. "Something to Sniff At," on page 156 is a real gem.

SPECIAL ARRANGEMENTS. All six of these tricks depend on the use of prearranged cards. Because of this, you should probably save them for opening tricks, or for occasions on which you're going to perform only one trick. Nothing looks more suspicious than taking out a different deck to perform a particular trick.

There is, however, a clever way in which you can switch decks. Assume you've just finished your routine with a superb trick. Put the cards in the card case, and put the case in your pocket. Suppose onlookers insist that you do more. Reach into that same pocket and remove a duplicate deck in which some of the cards have been set up. Perform one of the tricks from this section, followed by a few impromptu tricks.

ALL IN THE MIND. Here you have "mental" tricks. As part of your routine, you might choose a few of these. I find "You Might Wonder," on page 170 particularly arresting.

To begin with, fashion at least one fairly long routine and one short routine to use as a possible follow-up. Practice all these tricks until their performance is second nature to you. You'll feel confident and secure, and your performance will be polished and entertaining.

TRICKS

Strictly speaking, the following four tricks are forces—that is, you know the name of the "freely" chosen card in advance. They are, however, perfect for performing mental tricks. Apparently, a card is selected in the fairest possible way; yet you are able to read the spectator's mind and divine the name.

So with these four selections, you can either force the card for use in some other trick, or you may perform a feat of mind reading. If you decide to read a person's mind, you should reveal the name of the chosen card gradually—first revealing the color of the card, then the suit, and finally the value. In revealing the value, you apparently run into some confusion. For example, you know that the card is the ace of clubs. You have already divined the color and the suit. Concentrating fiercely, you say, "I can't seem to get the value. It looks like a 4. No, no! Not a 4. It looks *like* a 4. Let me see. It's an ace!" Pause. "The ace of clubs."

Similarly, you might at first confuse a 3 with an 8, or a 2 with a 5—any two cards that are moderately similar will do. Such nonsense is designed to convince spectators that mind reading is extremely difficult and seldom precise. Deep down, everyone *knows* that this is baloney. But just maybe …

The last three tricks in this category are not forces; rather, they are quite clever and certainly worthy of your consideration.

THE WAY BACK

Since the dirty work for this one is done behind your back, you'd better make sure no one is behind you.

One way or another, you must know the name of the top card. You can sneak a peek in advance, but I recommend this: Say, "I wonder if the joker is in here." Fan through the cards, apparently seeking the joker. The joker isn't there, but you do get a look at the top card of the deck.

Announce, "I'm going to attempt a feat of telepathy, so I don't guarantee any degree of success."

Place the deck face up onto the table. Gary knows his way around a deck of cards, so get him to assist you. Say, "Gary, please cut off a huge pile of cards and turn them over on the rest of the deck."

Gary lifts off a large number of face-up cards, turns them over, and sets them, face down, onto the remaining face-up cards.

ILLUS. 15

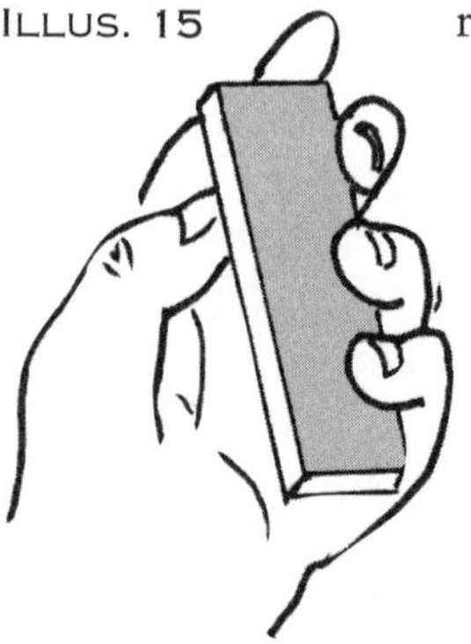

Continue, "Please cut off a smaller pile, turn it face up, and set it on top of the remaining cards."

He does it. You may tell him to cut off another small pile, turn it over, and set it back onto the remaining cards. In fact, this can be done several times.

"They should be pretty well mixed."

Pick up the cards with your right hand and place them in the dealing position in your left hand. The lowermost card is the one you sneaked a peek at.

Move your left hand behind your back. At the same time, turn away from the group. Your back is now to the group, the deck behind your back in your left hand.

"Gary, I'd like you to cut off a pile of cards. But please cut into the face-down cards so that no one else can see the card that you choose."

Gary cuts off a pile.

Turn back toward the spectators, keeping your left hand behind your back. The right hand remains in front of you where the group can see it.

Ask, "Did you cut into the face-down cards?"

At the same time, stick your left thumb underneath the pile and flip the cards over (Illus. 15).

Gary says yes.

Instantly turn around. Once again the spectators are looking at your back and the cards in your left hand.

"Gary, please look at the card you cut to. And show it to only one other person. I don't want anyone to think that one of the spectators is helping me." Pause. "When you're done, put the card back on top and put the rest of the cards on top of it. Then take the deck into your hands and concentrate on your card."

Naturally, the card Gary looks at is the original top card of the deck. Since you know the card, you can gradually read his mind.

OUT OF MY HANDS

You need to know the bottom card. This is relatively easy. You can sneak a peek as you pass the deck from hand to hand. Or you can tilt the deck forward and get a glimpse as you hand it to a spectator (Illus. 16).

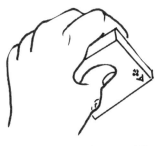

ILLUS. 16

Let's assume that Linda has agreed to help out. Hand her the deck, saying, "Please cut off a pile of cards and put it on the table."

She does.

"Turn over the top card of those you're holding. Put it, face up, on top of the cards on the table."

She does.

"Put the rest of the cards you're holding on top of those on the table."

She follows your instructions perfectly.

"Now, Linda, please pick up the deck and fan through the cards so that only you can see the faces. Fan to the card you turned over. The card right after that is your card. Remember the name of that card." Wait until she's ready. "Turn the face-down card over and give the deck a good shuffle."

Linda has looked at the original bottom card of the deck. With your usual dramatic presentation, read her mind.

My Variation

I recently read a book in which a simplified version of this really old principle was presented as a wonderful force. It would not fool a soul, of course. Who would be fooled? To paraphrase S. J. Perelman, "It's hard to imagine where you would find such a collection of addlepates and feebs."

Here is a variation that seems to fool people, however. You must know the name of the eighth card from the top of the deck.

Start by having Henry shuffle the deck. Take it back and turn it face up so that all can see the cards. Start fanning through the deck, saying, "The cards look pretty mixed up to me."

After fanning out ten cards or more, place these cards on top (the back of the deck). Fan through further. After you fan through several, take note of an inconspicuous card. Consider it as the first card as you go on fanning. Continue counting to yourself as you fan through the cards. (Count in threes; it's less obvious.) When you reach eight, place all the cards you've fanned on top (the back of the deck).

That inconspicuous card you noted is now eighth from the top of the deck.

Fan through another large group of cards, but don't place them on top; simply close these up.

Say these exact words to Henry: "Name a number between one and ten." Chances are very strong that he'll name either seven or eight. If he names seven, deal seven cards into a pile, counting aloud. Without saying anything, hold the deck out to Henry. Point to the top card. He takes it and looks at it.

If Henry says eight, hand him the deck and ask him to count down to the eighth card and look at it.

If he names a number from two to six, you simply subtract that number from 8. For instance, if Henry chooses five, you subtract 5 from 8, getting 3.

"Here's what I'd like you to do, Henry. Just count out your number, like this." As you utter the last sentence, deal three cards into a pile one by one. Drop the deck on top of the dealt cards. Pick up the entire deck and hand it to Henry. "Then look at the card that lies at your number."

He deals out five cards and then looks at the original eighth card from the top.

Similarly, if he chose the number two, you'd subtract 2 from 8, getting 6. This time you demonstrate by dealing six cards into a pile. Drop the deck on top of the six. Pick up the entire pile and hand it to Henry. Again he gets to choose the eighth card from the top.

Understand that you're not going to have to do this very often; most of the time Henry will choose either seven or eight.

But what if that sneaky guy chooses nine? Nothing to it: You resort to an old ruse. Spread out three cards from the top of the deck. Deal them onto the table into a loose pile, saying, "Three." Take two more and place them on top of those on the table, saying, "And two is five." Add two more, saying, "And two is seven." And toss on a final two, saying, "And two is nine."

Promptly even up the pile and place it on top of the deck. Extend the deck toward Henry, indicating that he should take the top card. That top card, of course, is actually the original eighth from the top.

Unless Henry is hearing impaired, he will not choose one or ten. After all, you *did* say "*between* one and ten."

Henry can put the deck together and shuffle the cards as you gradually read his mind.

Five-and-Ten

Following a similar principle to that mentioned in the previous force, get a known card to the *seventh* position from the top.

Ask Mary Lee to help out. Say to her, "Mary Lee, give a number between five and ten." The phrasing restricts her choices to six, seven, eight, and nine.

If the choice is six, deal off six cards one at a time and place the next card aside. If the choice is seven, hand her the deck, saying, "Please count down to the seventh card."

If the choice is eight, deal the cards by twos onto the table, one pair on top of the other. "Two, four, six, eight." Place the packet on top of the deck, and then stall for a moment. You might say something like, "You had complete freedom of choice of any number you wished." Extend the deck toward Mary Lee for the removal of the top card.

If the choice is nine, deal the cards in groups of three, saying, "Three, six, nine." Place the packet on top of the deck and follow the procedure indicated when the choice is eight.

In each instance, Mary Lee has chosen the original seventh card from the top. And, of course, you're delighted to read her mind.

Let's Prognosticate

This spectacular Michael Jeffreys invention is perfect, if you don't mind ruining a deck of cards. Let's assume that you're looking forward to a special occasion and that the guest of honor will be John Jones. Prepare a deck of cards like this: Count off 26 cards. With a marking pen, print *John Jones* on the back of all 26.

On the backs of the other 26, print a variety of names—making sure you include both first and last names. Place these face up onto the table. On top of them, place the *John Jones* cards face up. You're ready.

At the celebration, approach Mr. Jones. Remove the cards from your pocket so that they are face up.

"Mr. Jones, I wonder if you'd be kind enough to touch one of these cards."

Slowly fan the cards from the uppermost down. Jones should have no trouble touching one of the 26 John Jones cards.

If you feel daring, you might name the card selected, and then close up the cards. Say, "If you like, you might touch a different card. It's strictly up to you, sir."

Again fan through slowly, making sure he touches one of the John Jones cards.

But let's assume that you don't feel daring. Have Jones remove the card from the deck.

Turn the deck so that it's face down. Slowly fan through at least 20 cards from the top. "Notice, sir, that on the backs of the cards are different names."

Since you're showing the various names, progress through the deck will be quite slow. Jones should be happy when you stop after 20 cards.

Close up the deck and stick it into your pocket.

"Out of all those different names, I wonder which one you chose, sir."

Jones turns the card over. On the other side, of course, is his name.

Take the card from him. Remove the deck from your pocket and replace the card somewhere in the middle.

But won't Jones want to examine the deck? Maybe. Give it to him. On the backs of all the cards are different names. Really? Yes, you rapscallion. You took another deck and wrote on the backs of 26 cards all the names you had put down originally and added different names to the other 26. The trick deck was in your right-hand pocket originally. This deck was in your left-hand pocket. When you placed the trick deck in your left pocket, you simply released it and gripped the other deck. You then left your hand in your pocket as you said to Jones, "Out of all those different names, I wonder which you chose, sir."

Pause for a bit, giving Jones a chance to restore his senses. Then hold out your hand for the card as you remove the deck from your pocket.

It's a bit of trouble, but miracles aren't always easy.

Note

Suppose Jones examines the deck and notices that there is another card of the same value as the one he chose. Simple. Explain, "That's right. The one you chose is an extra card that I added to the deck. Amazing, eh?"

Two for One

Here we have two tricks that form a perfect routine. The first is the invention of Bob Hummer. Both tricks have appeared in other books of mine, but in this form they become twice as effective.

Part One

To start, you have the deck shuffled. Take the cards back and begin dealing them into a face-down pile, counting to yourself. After you've dealt ten cards, say to Angela, "Please tell me when to stop."

Continue counting as you deal. When Angela says "stop," cease dealing. *But* make sure you have an even number of cards on the table. If, for instance, she says "stop" as you deal down the fifteenth card, deal one more to make sure you have an even number.

Let's suppose that Angela stops you after you've dealt 22 cards. Set the deck aside and pick up the 22 cards. Rapidly fan off exactly half the number of cards—in this instance, 11. Turn these face up. Shuffle the entire packet.

Hand the packet to Angela. "While I turn my back, shuffle these cards. When you're done, place the cards in my hand."

Turn away. Place your left hand behind your back for the placement of the cards. When she's done shuffling, Angela places the cards on your hand. Turn around so that you once more face the group.

Quickly count off 11 cards from the top of the packet. Turn your left hand over so that it's palm down; your right hand remains palm up (Illus. 17). Bring both piles forward and set them down.

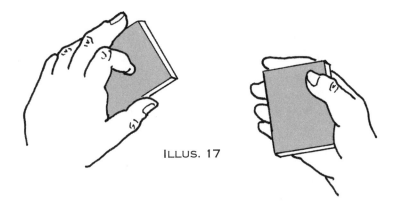

ILLUS. 17

Update: You have counted off half the cards. These are brought forward in the right hand. The bottom half is turned over, and this half is brought forward reversed in the left hand.

"In that short time, I have managed to put the same number of face-up cards in each pile."

The piles are examined. Sure enough, each contains the same number of face-up cards.

The trick is strengthened by a repetition.

<u>PART TWO</u>

"It's very strange, but somehow or other I seem to have control over face-up cards. Let's try another experiment, this time in precognition. To start, I'll make a prediction, using two cards."

Fan through the deck, making sure no one else can see the faces. Remove two cards and place them face down onto the table. The total should be somewhere between 15 and 20. Let's assume that you remove a 9 and an 8, the total being 17. "My prediction is the total of these two cards."

Hand the deck to Augie, turn away, and say, "Augie, please make two piles of cards, about a dozen in each pile. But you don't need to have the same number in each pile." Pause. "Pick up one of the piles and turn some cards face up. You may turn over a group of cards or turn over cards at different places." Pause. "Fan through that pile and see how many cards you've turned over." Pause. "Set that pile down and pick up the other pile. Turn over that same number of cards in that pile. You can turn them over wherever you wish in that pile also."

When he is done, continue, "Please put one of the piles on top of the deck and hide the other pile."

Put your hands behind your back and ask him to give you the deck.

With the cards behind your back, face the spectators and say, "Let's see if I can make my prediction come true." Count off from the top the number of cards in your prediction and turn them face up on top. In this instance, you would count off 17 cards and turn them face up on top. The quickest way to count off the cards is to take them one under the other.

Bring the cards forward and tell the spectator to place his other pile on top. "The question is," you say, "how many face-up cards do we now have?"

Fan through the deck, tossing out and counting aloud the face-up cards as you come to them. When your helper turns over your two prediction cards, he finds that the total precisely matches the number of face-up cards.

SOMETHING OLD, SOMETHING NEW

In Pensacola, Florida, I was fortunate enough to be able to associate with a wonderful group of magicians. Among them was John Braun, president of the local Society of American Magicians. At the meeting, John performed a clever variation of an old, old trick. Here it is, for your edification.

First, let me explain the original trick. Sneakily get a peek at the bottom card of the deck. Set the cards down on the table and ask Diane to cut off a pile. Point to the original bottom portion and say, "Please set these crosswise on top of the other pile." (See Illus. 18.)

ILLUS. 18

Provide a bit of time misdirection by making this sort of comment: "You cut the cards exactly where you wanted, right?" It doesn't much matter what you say, as long as it makes some kind of sense and eats up a little time.

Say, "Lift off the packet, please, and look at the card you cut."

Diane lifts off the top packet and looks at the card you previously peeked at. She concentrates on the card as you divine the suit and value bit by bit.

What did John add to the trick? He has someone shuffle the cards. If they are giving the deck an overhand shuffle, he says, "Go ahead, give them a good riffle-shuffle."

There's a good chance the spectator will riffle-shuffle the ends together, giving you a peek at the bottom card. If this happens, say, "Fine. Just set the cards onto the table, please."

If the person *doesn't* give you a peek, have someone else come up and give the cards a shuffle. You may have to try yet a third person. In fact, John had to wait till the third person shuffled the cards before he caught his glimpse.

As soon as you get your peek, step back and provide the

appropriate directions. Step away even farther as the spectator looks at the card and begins to concentrate.

A small variation, to be sure, but it makes the trick much more effective.

COINCIDENCE TRICKS

VERY LITTLE TURNOVER

How about a lively trick requiring no skill and with a wonderful surprise climax?

A little preparation is needed. Let's assume that you're going to use the two black queens. Put one face down on top. Turn the second card from the top face up. The third card is the other black queen, also face up.

Position from the top down: face-down black queen, any card face up, face-up black queen. (See Illus. 19.)

THIS IS THE QUEEN OF SPADES ON TOP OF THE DECK.

This should be your first trick. Remove the cards from the card case. Turn the deck face up. Fan through the face-up cards, saying, "Here we have an ordinary deck of marked cards." Stop before you get too close to the top.

Close up the cards, keeping them face up.

Marie is very agreeable, so she will undoubtedly agree to help out. "Marie, would you please cut off a pile of cards and place it face down onto the table."

She does.

"You may cut off more if you like, or put some back—whatever you choose."

Turn the remaining cards face up and place them right on top of the cards Marie cut off. "We'll just mark the spot."

So you have a face-down pile on the table, with a face-up pile on top of it.

Presumably you're marking the face-down pile with a face-up packet.

Why are you marking the spot? You have something very important to say: "Marie, was there any way at all that I could have influenced the spot at which you cut the cards?"

Of course not.

"Very well." Pick up the entire deck. Fan through the face-up cards until you come to the first face-down card. This is the queen that was originally third from the top of the deck. Below it is another face-down card. And below that is the other queen, face up.

Make sure you fan through the cards slowly enough so that you don't reveal the face-up queen.

Set the face-up cards onto the table. Hand Marie the face-down queen, again making sure you don't spread out the cards.

"Here's your chosen card, Marie."

Pick up the face-up cards on the table and place them face down on top of the deck. Presumably, the deck is now all face down.

"What card did you choose, Marie?"

She names it. Let's say that she got the queen of clubs.

"The queen of clubs? That's a very magical card. Please tap the top of the deck with it. Something wonderful might happen."

She taps the deck with the queen of clubs. You fan through the cards, showing that the queen of spades is face up.

"Good for you, Marie. You caused the exact sister of the queen of clubs to turn face up."

Who Has a Match?

You may prefer this trick, based on the principle used in the trick just described.

As before, a bit of preparation is necessary. Remove from the deck two cards of the same value and color, plus an indifferent card. Let's suppose that you remove from the deck the black sixes. Place one 6 face up on top of the deck. On top of this, place the indifferent card face up. On top of all goes the other black 6 face down.

The position: a black 6 face down on top, below it a face-up card, below that a face-up black 6.

Take the deck from the card case. Turn it face up.

Ask Tim to assist you. Fan through several cards from the bottom, letting Tim see the cards. Explain, "I have reversed one card in the deck. I wonder if you can, somehow, figure out which one it is. Let's start by having you cut off a packet of cards. To keep everything aboveboard, we'll have you cut from the face-up cards."

After he has cut off a group, say, "Is this how many you want? You can replace those and try again if you wish."

When he is done, have him place his cut-off pile *face down* onto the table. You're still holding a packet of face-up cards. Place this packet face up on top of the face-down pile on the table, saying, "So that's exactly the number of cards you want." Your cards should be set on top so that they're offset a bit, as in Illus. 20.

"Remember now, we're looking for you to somehow identify the one face-up card in the deck."

Pick up both piles together, closing them up as you do so. Fan down through the face-up cards to the first face-down card. (Go slowly near the end, so that you don't fan out too many cards and reveal the true position.)

Set the face-up cards aside for the moment. Carefully remove the top card of those you're holding and place it face down before Tim.

Pick up the pile you just placed on the table and put it on top of the cards you're holding. Put the combined pile face down onto the table.

"Let's review. I put one card face up into the deck. You cut the cards exactly where you wished." Tap the card before Tim. "And here's the card you chose. Let's find the face-up card."

Fan through the deck to the face-up 6—let's say the 6 of clubs. Take it out and place it next to Tim's card.

"And which card did you choose, Tim? Turn it over, please."

He turns over the 6 of spades.

"Unbelievable! You selected the perfect match."

IT'S ALL UP TO YOU

Helen always displays an extraordinary interest in how you perform your tricks. It's time that she tried a little magic herself.

Hand Helen the deck, saying, "I'd like you to do a card trick for me, Helen. First, so no one will be suspicious, you should give the cards a good shuffle."

When she's done, continue, "Now fan out the cards in front of me so that I can see the faces. When I see one I like, I'll take it out."

Note the top two cards. If Helen fans right by them, spread the top several cards yourself so that you can get a look at the top two. Let's suppose that the top two are the 3 of clubs and the 4 of hearts. You are going to find a card that combines the two. In other words, you will choose either the 3 of hearts or the 4 of clubs. It doesn't matter which. Let's say that you pick out the 3 of hearts.

Take your selected card from the deck and set it face down onto the table.

"Close up the cards, please, Helen."

She does.

"Now you should do something mysterious, like deal the cards into a pile."

She deals about ten cards into a pile.

"And you should stop dealing whenever you feel like it."

Eventually, she stops dealing.

"Excellent. You'd better set the rest of the deck aside."

She does.

"Let's make it really complicated. Take your pile and deal it into *two* piles. First, deal a card here ..." Indicate a spot on the table. "... and then a card here." Point to a spot next to the first spot. "Then continue dealing alternately, making two piles."

She does.

"Well, I can't think of anything else, Helen. Can you?"

No, she says. But if she does make a suggestion, negate it, saying, "No, I think that's a little too complicated."

Continue: "Let's see...why don't you turn over the top card of each pile?"

She does.

"I'll be darned," you declare, "a heart and a 3. In other words, a 3 of hearts."

Turn over the card you chose.

Note

If the top two cards are of the same value or suit, tell Helen, "I think the cards should be shuffled some more, Helen." She shuffles, and everything is fine. But suppose the two top cards are again of the same value or suit. Tell her the same thing. This could be very humorous, since everyone assumes that you're just being amusing.

ANOTHER WAY

Let's follow that up with a trick with a similar climax, but a much different method.

This time, let's work our magic on Raymond. Hand the deck to Raymond, asking him to shuffle. When he's done, take the deck, saying, "I'll have to find the perfect card for you to stick into the deck."

With the cards face up, quickly fan through to the end, noting the top card. Also, take a look at the bottom card. Let's

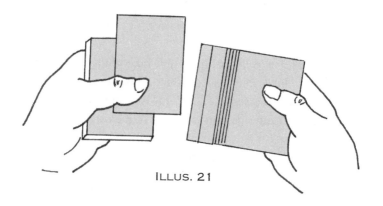

ILLUS. 21

suppose that the top card is the 8 of clubs, and the bottom card is the ace of hearts. You need to combine the value of one of these with the suit of the other. Look through the deck and remove either the 8 of hearts or the ace of clubs. Let's assume that you take out the ace of clubs. Hand the card, face down, to Raymond.

"This should be an absolutely suitable card for you to stick into the deck. Please push it into the deck part way."

Hold the deck out face down. Raymond sticks the card partially into the deck. Naturally, since you handed him the card face down, he sticks it into the deck face down.

"I'm sorry, Raymond, it's supposed to be face up."

Fan down to the protruding card with both hands palm up. Separate the right hand from the left (Illus. 21). On top of the cards in the left hand is the card that Raymond just pushed into the deck. Turn the left hand palm down. This brings these cards face up (Illus. 22). Put the protruding card face up on top of the face-down cards in the right hand. The right thumb assists in taking the card (Illus. 23).

Turn the left hand palm up. The cards in the left hand are now face down and the ace of clubs is face up on top of the face-down cards in the right hand. Place the cards that are in your left hand face down on top of the face-up selection.

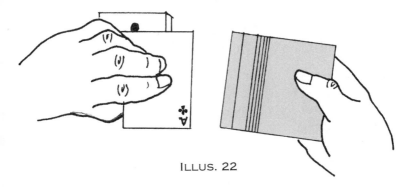

ILLUS. 22

It all seems very natural. But the face-up card is now between the original top and bottom cards.

Set the deck down. It's time to help the group forget about what just happened and to build to a climax.

"Raymond, you could have stuck your card in anywhere. But you chose that particular spot. Let's see if you managed to accomplish anything really mysterious."

Pick up the deck. Fan through and remove, in a group of

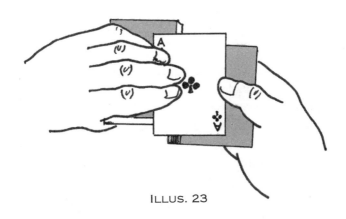

ILLUS. 23

ILLUS. 24

three, the face-up card and the card on either side of it. Set the three cards onto the table (Illus. 24).

"You shoved the ace of clubs into the deck. Let's see the other two cards."

Turn over the other two cards.

Tap the club. "Here we have the 8 of clubs, and your card is a club."

Tap the ace of hearts. "Here we have the ace of hearts, and your card is an ace."

Tap the ace of hearts. "Ace of ..." Tap the 8 of clubs. "... clubs."

Pause. "I can't believe it, Raymond. You found the two cards that match your card. Good going!"

JUST A LITTLE MORE

I worked out a variation on the preceding trick that is very effective. Perhaps you'll like it also.

Tracy plays bridge quite often, so she would be the perfect assistant. Hand her the deck and ask her to give it a good shuffle.

Take the cards back, saying, "Tracy, I'd like you to name any card at all."

After some thought, she names a card. Let's say that she names the king of spades.

"I'll find it for you."

Start fanning through the deck, faces toward yourself. After fanning out 20 cards or so, cut the cards you've fanned off to the top. This is to throw off suspicion when you cut the cards later.

Continue fanning. You're looking for a king (other than the king of spades) with a spade on one side of it. Your chances are excellent. When you find the match you're looking for, cut between the cards. This puts a king on the top and a spade on the bottom, or vice versa.

Start all over, fanning through the deck, this time really looking for the king of spades. When you find it, take it out of the deck. Hold it up so that all can see the face. Hand the card to Tracy *face down*.

"Here's your card, Tracy. Please push it into the deck part way."

She puts the card in face down. As in the previous trick, you turn the card face up, and eventually show that she has located two cards that match her selection.

This is quite a powerful effect, so I recommend that you don't fool with it. If, for example, you can't find a spade and a king together, *don't* fiddle with the cards, trying to arrange them properly. Instead, perform the previous trick. Hand the deck to Tracy, saying, "I have a better idea, Tracy. Shuffle the deck, and then *I'll* pick out a card for you to use."

Continue performing "Another Way," on page 43.

DYNAMIC DUO

This clever trick was developed by Bill Martin and mathematical wizard Martin Gardner.

A bit of preparation is necessary. Remove from the deck one card of each value—the suits are irrelevant. Set these up so the highest card (king) is on top and the lowest (ace) is on the bottom. Place the rest of the deck on top of these. The result is that the bottom 13 cards are set up like this:

K Q J 10 9 8 7 6 5 4 3 2 A

The ace is the bottom card.

You're ready to roll.

You'll need someone to assist you who will do a good job of riffle-shuffling the cards, so you'd better select Edith, who plays bridge nearly every afternoon.

Set the deck onto the table. Say to Edith, "Please cut off about half the cards, Edith."

She does.

"Now give those a good shuffle."

She shuffles.

"Turn your packet face up, Edith. Hold that in one hand. Take the other packet *face down* in the other hand. Now riffle-shuffle the two packets together."

When she finishes, there should be a fairly even mix of face-up and face-down cards. Take the deck from Edith and fan out the cards so that she can see the cards that were originally face down, including your setup.

"I think the cards are well mixed."

She will not notice the setup.

Spread the deck out on the table so that your setup is face down. Make sure that all the cards near the bottom are spread out so that you can tell all the cards in your face-down setup. As you will see, this is quite important.

"Edith, please look over the face-up cards and pick out any one you wish."

She picks a card. Have her place it aside on the table. Let's suppose that she chooses a 3.

"Let's see if I can pick a good card."

Count *up* to the third face-down card from the bottom. It, too, is a 3. Remove it and place it face down next to Edith's choice.

"Pick another one, Edith."

She does. Have her place it a little distance from her first choice. If she takes a card of the same value as her first choice, tell her, "No, you've already taken one of those, Edith. Try something different."

But she's very cooperative today, so say, "That's an excellent card. Maybe *I* can find a good one also."

Again count from the bottom to a card that will match

Edith's. (If the second card is higher than the first, you will have to count to one card less than the value of Edith's selection.) Place this card next to Edith's second choice.

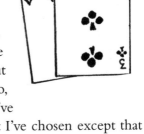

Gather up the cards on the table, placing the face-up cards face down. You don't want to leave any evidence of your setup. As you do this, chat about the present situation. You might say, "So, you've chosen two cards, Edith, and I've chosen two cards. I have no idea what I've chosen except that I had a strong feeling that they were good cards. Did you have that same feeling about the ones that you picked?" She responds. "Well, let's see what we accomplished."

Turn over your first choice, placing it partially on Edith's card (Illus. 25). "My goodness, they match. Let's check the other one."

Turn over your second choice and, as before, place it on Edith's second choice.

"Two matches! You did an incredible job, Edith."

Location Tricks

Don't Take That Tone with Me

There's nothing wrong with an old-time trick—especially a good one. And more especially, if you can patch it up a bit and give it a new lease on life. Here's one that's a real fooler.

You'll need to prepare a little. Remove all the clubs from the deck. Place six on top of the deck and seven on the bottom. Take any three cards from the middle of the deck and put them on the bottom.

Since Paul is quite the wheeler-dealer, start by handing him the deck and saying, "Paul, please deal out six cards in a face-down row."

He does (Illus. 26).

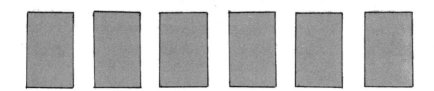

ILLUS. 26

"In the same way, deal another six on top of them. Then just continue on, all the way through the deck."

When Paul gets to the last four cards, tell him, "Just set those aside, Paul. We won't need them."

If he has already dealt one or two of the four on top of the piles, just pick them off the piles and add them to those Paul has already set aside.

On the table are six eight-card piles. A club is at the top and bottom of each pile.

"I'm going to turn away, Paul. While I'm not watching,

please take a card from the middle of any of the piles. Look at it and show it around."

Turn your back while Paul does his duty.

"Now place that card on top of any one of the piles. Then gather up the piles one on top of the other … in any order you wish."

Paul is done at last. Turn back to the group. Have Paul give the deck a complete cut. Others may cut the deck as well.

"Believe it or not, Paul, through years of experience I can tell when a person names his chosen card. Now that's no great trick if I ask you to name your card and then say, 'Yep, that's your card.' Nor would it be wonderful if I told you to name three cards with one of them being your chosen card. After all, one out of three isn't so great. But I'm going to ask you to name all the cards in the deck one by one, and—from the tone of your voice—I'll be able to tell your chosen card. Come to think of it, you may not have to go all the way through the deck. Would you start naming the cards, please, Paul. You can go fairly fast."

Of course he can. You're listening to hear clubs named. Chances are, he'll mention two clubs in a row at least once before he gets to the chosen card. How can you tell when he gets there? Easy. He'll mention a club, another card, and then another club. That card between the two clubs is the one chosen.

Paul might say, "7 of hearts, 8 of spades, 2 of clubs, 3 of diamonds, 6 of clubs, 9 of hearts, queen of …"

"Did you say 3 of diamonds?"

"Yes, I did."

"Just as I thought. That's your card."

DOUBLE DISCOVERY

Charles Jordan, I think, came up with the original idea. It has been expanded on by many writers, but the original idea is still very strong. I have added a few notions which lead the spectators to believe that two chosen cards are hopelessly lost.

Start by handing the deck to Estelle and asking her to shuffle the cards. When she finishes, ask Claude to take the deck. "Please deal quite a few cards into a pile, Claude. Stop whenever you wish."

As he deals, pretend to pay no attention. Actually, count the cards mentally. For, in a moment, Estelle will turn a card face up and place it into this group. The number of face-down cards *must* be even.

So if you mentally count 21, for instance, you say to Estelle, "Please pick up the pile that Claude just dealt out. Turn one of the cards face up—any card you wish." Now an even number of cards is face down and one card is face up.

Suppose Claude deals out 20 cards—an even number. Say to Estelle, "Please take the rest of the deck from Claude. Take any card from this group. Turn the card face up and add it to the group that Claude just dealt out." Again, an even number of cards is face down and one card is face up.

ILLUS. 27

ESTELLE REMEMBERS THIS CARD.

One way or the other, you must remember the number of face-down cards. The remainder of the deck is set aside.

"That face-up card is going to help each of you choose a card."

Have each spectator shuffle the packet. Take the cards and fan down to the face-up card. Tilt the cards up so that Estelle can see the faces (Illus. 27). "Estelle, I'd like you to remember the card that's on my side of the card you stuck into the deck. In other words, look at the card that's face to face with that card." Make sure she remembers the right card.

Let Claude see the faces of the cards. "Claude, I'd like you to remember the card that's on your side of the card that Estelle stuck into the deck. In other words, look at the card that's back to back with that card." Make sure that he gets a good look at the right card.

"Please don't forget your cards; that would ruin everything." Set the packet onto the table. "Now I'd like each of you to give the packet a complete cut."

They do so.

You pick up the packet, saying, "I think I'd better mix them up even more."

You're about to perform the "Up-and-Down Shuffle," described on page 19. In this instance, pass the cards from your left hand to your right, one at a time. Push the top card upward, the second one down, the third card upward, the fourth down, and so on through the packet. When you're done, strip out the lower section of cards (second, fourth, sixth, and so on). Place this section on top of the other section. Even up the cards. Set the pile onto the table. Alternatively, you push the first card *downward*, the next card *upward*, and so on. And, after you strip out the lower section of cards, you may place this section on top.

Now that you know how to do the shuffle, continue: "I'm going to give the cards an up-and-down shuffle. Estelle, should I push the top card up or down?"

Do whatever she indicates. The next card goes in the opposite direction, and so on. You strip out the lower section.

Turn to Claude. Indicate the pile you stripped out, saying, "Should I place these on top or on the bottom of the others?" Do whatever he says.

"It might be a good idea to have the cards mixed a little more. How about each one of you giving the cards one more cut."

They do.

"We'd better try another up-and-down shuffle."

Again, let Estelle choose whether the first card should go up or down, and let Claude pick whether the stripped-out cards should go above or below the others.

Set the packet onto the table and invite Estelle and Claude to cut the cards yet again.

After they finish, pick up the packet and fan through it, passing the face-down cards from your left hand to your right. When you come to the face-up card, place the cards that are in your right hand onto the table. The face-up card is on top of the cards remaining in your left hand (Illus. 28).

"We won't need this card any more," you say.

Take the card with your right hand and place it with the discarded remainder of the deck. With your right hand, take the cards remaining in your left hand and place them onto the packet on the table.

In effect, at that point, you have removed the face-up card and cut the cards.

One of the selected cards is at the same number from the top of the packet as the other is from the bottom of the packet. And you know what the number is.

You know the total number of cards in the packet—in our example, 20. Divide this number by 4. If the number won't divide evenly by 4, add 2 to it and then divide by 4. Suppose the number is 18. You divide 18 by 4, but it will not divide evenly. You add 2 to 18, giving you 20, which divided by 4 is 5. So the selected cards are 5 from the top and 5 from the bottom.

Suppose the packet contains 28 cards. You divide by 4, getting 7. The selected cards are 7 from the top and 7 from the bottom.

There are many ways in which you can reveal the cards. My favorite method is to milk the cards—that is, taking the top and bottom cards together and placing them into a pile. (See "Milking the Cards," page 18.) Repeat the procedure. Continue fairly rapidly until you're three deals from the chosen two. Suppose that the chosen cards are at the seventh position. Milk the cards four times rapidly. Stop and say to both assistants, "Tell me when to stop, please."

Fairly slowly, deal one and then another. If someone says "stop" at this point, you milk the next two but continue to hold them. Set the rest of the packet down. The top card of the two is Claude's; the other is Estelle's.

Ask Claude to name his card. He names it and you show it. Ask Estelle to name hers; sure enough, you also have her card.

If neither says "stop" when you've dealt off the next two, look at the couple inquiringly. If neither responds, say, "How about these two cards?" If one or both utter an affirmative, proceed as described above. If not, say, "I think they might do." Set the cards in your hand aside. Pick up the two chosen cards and proceed as described.

With two persons involved, you have an excellent chance of one of them stopping you appropriately. But if not, it's still quite an astonishing trick.

Note

As you have undoubtedly figured out, it doesn't matter what decisions are made on the up-and-down shuffles. If you perform two shuffles, everything will turn out properly.

Another way to finish is to turn the packet face up and begin milking the cards. Say, "If one of you sees your card, please stop me." When you are stopped, show that the lower card is also a chosen one.

THE LONG COUNT

I am convinced that there's nothing wrong with trying to revive a wonderful device that has been terribly neglected for the past several decades. I'm referring to the "faced deck." That is, unbeknownst to the spectators, the upper half of the deck is face down and the lower half is face up.

But before you "face" the deck, there's quite a bit more to do. Start off by having someone shuffle the deck. Sam is always helpful, so ask him to give a hand.

He shuffles the cards thoroughly and gives the deck back.

"Now, Sam, I'd like you to think of a number from one to five. Got one?"

He does.

"I'll show you the cards one by one. Please note the card that lies at your number. And—here comes the tough part—please remember both your card and the number."

Avert your head. Hold up the top card so that Sam can see it. Announce, "One."

Take the next card from the deck. Hold it *in front* of the first card as you show it to Sam. Say, "Two."

The third card goes in front of the other two. Show it to Sam and say, "Three."

Continue until you've shown the top five cards, announcing each number as you show it.

Because of the way you've shown the cards, the top five go back on top in the same order as they were before.

It's time to ask Angie to also help out.

"Angie, please think of a number from ten to 20. Do you have one?" She does. "Good. I'm now going to put the deck behind my back and make a certain clever arrangement."

Place the cards behind your back. Turn the top half face up and place it on the bottom. The half in which Sam's card lies is now face up below the face-down half. Bring the deck forward. Be careful not to tilt it upward so that spectators can see the bottom card.

"First of all, Sam, let me show you that your card is no longer at its original number. What number did you pick?"

Suppose he says four. You deal off four cards into a face-down pile. Turn over the last card dealt, showing that it is not Sam's card.

"Angie, what number did you choose?"

She names her number. Let's suppose that it's 13. Mentally subtract Sam's number from Angie's number. In this instance, you'd subtract 4 from 13, getting 9.

You have already dealt four cards from the top and turned over the fourth card, proving that it's not the chosen one. Say, "All right, this is number four." Turn the card face down. Continue dealing, saying aloud, "five, six, seven, eight, nine."

You have stopped as the result of subtracting Sam's number from Angie's. Drop your left hand to your side. At the same time, tap the ninth card, saying, "That's my lucky number." Turn over the ninth card. Look at Sam and say, "I hope it didn't turn out to be your selected card."

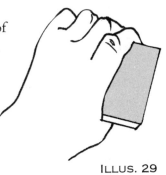

ILLUS. 29

As you almost complete the sentence, bring the hand back up, only with the palm down (Illus. 29). You have reversed the deck. The half containing Sam's card is now in the top face-down pile. As you converse with the pile, take the deck into your palm-up right hand. Then casually place it into your left hand, in the dealer's position.

Turn the ninth card face down, saying, "So that's nine." Continue dealing, saying aloud, "Ten, 11, 12, 13. Thirteen was your number, right Angie?"

Right.

"And what was your card, Sam?"

He names it. You turn over card number 13, the last one you dealt out. Somehow you have managed to bring Sam's card to the number chosen by Angie.

Review

1) Sam thinks of a number from one to five. You show him the first five cards, numbering them aloud. Sam is to remember his number and the card that lies at that number. The five cards are returned to the deck in their original order.

2) Angie thinks of a number from ten to 20.

3) You put the deck behind your back. The top half is placed face-up on the bottom.

4) Bring the deck back to the front. Ask Sam his number. Deal that many cards into a pile. Show that his card is no longer at that number.

5) Ask Angie for her number. Subtract Sam's number from Angie's number. Suppose Sam chose three and Angie chose 17. Subtract 3 from 17, getting 14. You have already dealt out three cards. Continue dealing to 14, which happens to be your lucky number. As this card is revealed, you drop your hand and bring it back up, reversing the deck.

6) Continue the deal to 17. Show that the seventeenth card is Sam's.

Note

The deck is still faced; how do you fix it?

Do a trick requiring that a card be chosen. Fan out the top several cards, asking a spectator to choose one. If the spectator is unreceptive and seems intent on taking a card farther down in the deck, choose someone else.

Once the card is chosen, turn away, saying, "Please show the card to the rest of the group."

Your back is to the group; you might as well straighten out the deck. Turn back and complete your trick.

IMPROMPTU LIAR'S TRICK

A card is chosen and returned to the deck. The magician asks the spectator to name a color—either red or black. The spectator may give the same color as the chosen card or a different color. The magician spells out the answer, dealing out one card from the deck for each letter in the spelling. The card on the last letter of the spelling is turned over; it is the same color as that of the chosen card—regardless of whether the spectator has lied or told the truth.

The same procedure is followed for the suit and value of the chosen card. At last the final card is turned over. It is the chosen card.

A wonderful trick, and, in most instances, it requires a modest setup of the deck. But here we have my invention, a sort of satirical version of the same trick.

Don's reputation is that he's very good at exaggeration, so he'd be the ideal helper for this trick. Hand him the deck and ask him to give the cards a good shuffle.

Have Don choose a card and return it, using the method described in "Simplicity Itself," on page 11. This means that you know the card above the one chosen.

Turn the deck so that the faces are toward you. Fan through

it until you come to the "key" card—the one just beyond the chosen card. *Starting with the key card*, count eleven cards as you continue fanning through the face-up deck. Your best bet is to count the cards in threes and, after you have counted nine, add two more cards to those in your right hand.

Separate the cards after counting eleven. Tilt the deck down so that all can see the faces of the cards. Place the cards that are in your right hand below those in the left hand, so that when the deck is face down, the cards that were in your right hand would be on top. Even up the cards.

The result is that the chosen card is now twelfth from the top of the deck. But, after the cut, keep the cards face up, for you are about to offer the goofiest excuse ever for fanning through the cards.

"See this card?" you say, calling attention to the card at the face of the deck. All can see the card. "I can tell you right now that this is *not* your card." Pause, as though waiting for approval. "Now if I could do that 50 more times, we'd have a *real* trick. But let's try something else."

Turn the deck face down. "Let's play the liar's game. The liar's game is to lie sometimes and to tell the truth at other times so that no one else can tell the difference. Sound exciting? You bet. I'm going to ask you some questions, Don, and when you answer, you can either lie or tell the truth—whatever you want. Ready?"

He is.

"Is your card red or black—lie or tell the truth."

It doesn't matter what he says. If he says red, you spell it out, dealing one card face down for each letter in the spelling, forming a pile on the table. If he says black, you say, "Maybe yes, maybe no. I'm going to spell red." And you proceed to spell out red, as described.

"Let's see what we got." Turn over the next card. Whatever the color is, name it and say, "Just as I thought." Place the card face down onto the pile.

Pause. "Name a suit, Don. You can name the actual suit of your card, or some other suit. Clubs, hearts, spades, or diamonds—what do you pick?"

He names a suit. If he names clubs, you say, "Excellent!" Spell it out, adding the cards to the top of the pile. If he names another suit, say, "Oh, sure! Well, I'll just spell out clubs." Proceed to spell it out.

You turn over the next card and comment on it. Here is where your ability to ad-lib will sparkle. It doesn't really matter what you say, but it should have some relevance to the card turned over. If it turns out to be a club, fine. Say, "Just as I expected."

If it's a spade, and Don named something different, you might say, "See? I knew it would be a black card."

If it's a red card, you might comment, "Notice, Don, that we got the *opposite* color. Now we're getting somewhere."

Turn the card face down on top of the pile. "Was your card high or low, Don—lie or tell the truth?"

Whatever Don says, you say, "It definitely is a low card, so we'll spell out 'low.'"

Turn over the next card. To some extent, your remarks will be based on what you've said previously. For example, if you previously mentioned that you got the opposite color, you might either say, "Ah, naturally, we once more have the opposite—a low card, rather than a high card," or, "Ah, naturally—just as I predicted—we get a low card this time." If the card is what Don mentioned, you could say, "Congratulations, Don—exactly as you said."

In each instance, you have something to say. The idea is to pretend that each card that you turn up is exactly what you expected. Sometimes there is a certain logic to it all. For instance, on occasion, every single card you turn over will be inaccurate—which seems to be your exact intention. Sometimes, every card you turn over will match the spectator's choice—which is *real* magic.

Now comes some real sneakiness. If you ask Don to choose the value of a card, chances are strong that the choice will be 7, 8, or—occasionally—3. All three of these are spelled with five letters.

And you have two additional chances: (1) Don may name queen, which is also spelled with five letters. (2) he may name five, which can simply be counted out, rather than spelled.

"We should start getting a little more truthful, don't you think, Don? At least *I* should get more truthful. Name the value of a card, Don. Again, it could be the same as your card, or it could be a lie."

Quite often, Don will name 7, 8, or 3. And perhaps he'll choose queen or 5. If he happens to choose one of these, continue, "As I say, let's deal out your exact choice." Spell out the value, and turn over the next card.

But suppose Don is not quite normal and chooses a different value, such as 4. Say, "Oh, what a silly choice, Don. Let's try lucky 7." Spell out seven, and turn over the next card.

If the card turns out to be of the same value as Don named, you obviously have a miracle feat. If it turns out to be the same value as the one *you* chose, you also have a miracle feat. Remember when you fanned through the deck to bring Don's selected card twelfth from the top? Well, the card *before* the key card is the selected card. If your memory is pretty good, you could make a mental note of the value of the chosen card. Once in a great while, this will come in handy. For instance, you count down five cards and turn over the next and it turns out to be the same value as the one selected. If this happens, say something like this: "My goodness, it *is* time for the truth. Here we have a card that's exactly the same value as the one you chose."

Suppose that the card is the same suit as the selected card. "A heart. Oh, sure! *Now* we get a card of the same suit as the one you chose."

This might make the trick even stronger, but you don't

really have to note the selected card. Nevertheless, you absolutely must make some sort of comment, just as you've done the other three times. You might comment on the card's relationship to the spectator's choice or your choice. For instance, if the card is a 4 and the spectator chose 6, you could say, "You chose 6 and this card is a 4. Amazing! They're both even numbers." Or you could be amazed that you chose an odd number and that the card is also odd. Or you could be absolutely flabbergasted that you both chose an odd number, yet the card is even—what a coincidence!

As you can see, what you say doesn't have to be clever; it just has to be prompt.

Turn the card face down on top of the pile. *Pick up the pile and place it on top of the deck.* As you're doing this, say, "It's time for the truth, Don. Both you and I have to be truthful, alright?"

Of course it is.

"So we'll spell out … *the truth.*"

Spell out *the truth* exactly as you did the other words. Take the next card from the deck and hold it out face down. "The truth now, Don. What was the name of your card?"

He names it. You turn it over. It's the chosen card.

"I knew this would work. Remember, I told you that this is the liar's game? Well, nobody's a better liar than I am."

The truth is … you're terrific.

Notes

1) Here are the words you spell out, in order:

(color): RED
(suit): CLUBS
(low or high): LOW
(value): SEVEN (also possible: EIGHT, THREE, QUEEN)
THE TRUTH

2) Hard to believe, but with all the counting, a couple of cards could get stuck together or something else could go wrong.

In the unlikely event that this occurs and you end up with the wrong card, you might say, "As I said, we need the truth. And to tell you the truth, I don't know why I even tried that trick." Immediately swing into a trick that will work.

3) When you read this long description, you might get the impression that this trick is difficult. It's not. Yes, you'll need to run through it several times before trying it out on friends and then strangers. But once you master it, you'll find that it's quite easy and moves along rapidly.

WHAT ELSE?

Dave Altman seems to specialize in tricks with unusual endings. Here is one I think you'll like.

The only requirement is that you get a peek at the top card. You might try the method recommended at the beginning of "The Way Back," on page 27. Be sure to remember that top card, for it's your key card.

To begin, pick out someone who plays enough cards to be able to give the deck a good riffle-shuffle. Andy would be perfect.

Set the deck onto the table. Tell Andy, "Please cut off about half the cards. Look at the card you cut off and show it around."

Andy shows his friends the bottom card of the packet he cut off.

You turn your back and continue: "Please turn the cards on the table face up. Now do one riffle-shuffle, shuffling the *face-down* cards into the *face-up* cards. When you're done, set the deck onto the table." Pause. "Is the deck on the table? Good. Give the deck a complete cut."

You can have it cut again if you wish.

Turn back to the group. Pick up the deck and turn it over. Spread out the cards so that all can be seen. Both your key card and the chosen card will be among the face-up cards.

As you spread the cards, note your key card. Following it

will be a face-down card, or perhaps several face-down cards. But the first face-up card beyond it is the chosen card. Don't pause at it, of course, but be sure to remember it.

Let me quote Dave:

"Now comes the fun. To reveal the spectator's card, have the spectator pull out from the tabled fan four face-down cards that he *feels* have some connection with the noted card. The magician turns them face up and, whatever their value/suit/pictures, uses them to pinpoint the noted card.

"For example, assume that the noted card is the 7 of spades, and the four cards selected are 10 of spades, jack of hearts, king of diamonds, and 3 of spades. Discard the two face cards, explaining that they have no numerical value. Point out that the two remaining cards are spades, and that 3 subtracted from 10 equals 7, so that the noted card must be the 7 of spades! Congratulate the spectator on picking out the four appropriate cards."

Dave gives another example: The noted card is the queen of clubs, and the four pulled-out cards are 4 of diamonds, queen of hearts, 9 of spades, and ace of diamonds.

Say, "You'll notice that only one of these cards is a picture card, the queen. Also, every suit is represented except clubs. Therefore, the chosen card must be the queen of clubs."

Dave tells us, "The more ridiculous or far-fetched the pinpointing, the more the fun. Enjoy, and don't forget to congratulate the spectator."

Notes

1) Obviously, if you wish, you can eliminate Dave Altman's clever ending and simply locate the selected card and name it, or produce it in some other way.

2) I really like Dave's method of locating the chosen card. But, if you prefer, you can simply force a card and use Dave's method of revealing the name. (See the first four tricks under the heading "Mental Tricks," from pages 27 to 38.)

PILES OF MAGIC

To perform this trick, you must be able to get a sneaky peek at the bottom card of the deck. I find it fairly easy to do as I riffle-shuffle the deck while standing up. Others may prefer to simply tilt the deck a bit while chatting with spectators. Yet others might find it convenient to turn the deck face up and quickly spread the cards, saying, "Note that it's an ordinary deck." In the process, they take note of the bottom card.

Now that you know the bottom card, you're ready for Evelyn to assist you. "Think of a number from two to ten, Evelyn." She does. "Please remember that number."

Turn away from the group.

"Evelyn, please look at the card that lies at your number from the top. Let everyone else see that card. Be sure to keep that card at your number from the top."

When Evelyn is ready, continue, "Evelyn, please give the deck a complete cut."

She does.

"You're about to deal out some cards, Evelyn. When you do, deal them slowly and quietly so that I'll have no idea as to the number. Now start by dealing into a row the same number of cards as your number from the top. For example, if your number were 3, you'd deal three cards into a row, from left to right. Be sure to take a little extra time so that I won't get the number."

She finishes.

"Now please wait till I complete all these directions. In the same way as you dealt before, deal out one more card on top of each one you dealt out. Continue dealing like this until all the deck is dealt out. You can start now. Let me know when you're done."

When she's done, continue: "Gather up the piles, one on top of the other, in any order you wish."

Finally Evelyn announces that she's finished. You turn back

to the group and take the deck. Fan through with the faces toward yourself. The card to the left of the one you peeked at is the chosen card. In other words, as you fan through the face-up deck, the chosen card is the one immediately after the one you peeked at. Remove the selected card from the deck and place it face down onto the table. Ask Evelyn to name her card. When she does, you turn over the selection.

It hardly seems possible, but the method of dealing always ensures that the card you peeked at will be on top of the selected card.

Meet Madam Flaboda

You go through a bit of business at the beginning of this trick; after this, the spectator handles the cards throughout. Apparently, the trick can't possibly work. But it certainly does, and quite amusingly.

My friend Wally Wilson has a mysterious invisible acquaintance named Madam Flaboda. She frequently helps him with his magic tricks. Here we have an excellent example. I have changed the working slightly.

Incidentally, I present two possible ways to present the beginning portion of the trick. The one I present first is simple and deceptive. The other method, which is also quite effective, appears in the note at the end of the trick.

To start, you must have a full deck. Have Gloria shuffle the cards. Take the deck back and turn it face up.

"The cards are well mixed, as you can see."

Fan through the face-up cards, mentally counting them in threes. When you reach 18, separate the two face-up groups, holding one section in each hand. Turn to Gloria, saying, "You did an excellent job, Gloria."

Set the pile of 18 cards onto the table face down. Set the remainder of the deck face down next to it. Point to this pile, saying, "Please cut off a pile, Gloria, and put it on the table."

She does.

"Nice job, Gloria. Now let's select a pile together. First, I'll take a pile."

Pick up one of the piles that does not contain the 18 cards.

"Now you take one."

If Gloria picks up the 18-card pile, say, "Excellent," and proceed with the trick. If she picks the other pile, hold out your empty hand. She gives you the pile. Indicate the 18-card pile. "Please pick it up."

Set the piles you're holding back onto the table.

Gloria is now holding the 18-card pile. You tell her to take it and shuffle it. Add, "Please take a look at the top card of the pile. Then set the pile onto the table."

She is then told to pick up one of the other piles, pick it up, shuffle it, and place it on top of the one she just placed on the table. She is also to shuffle the third pile and place it on top of all.

The chosen card is now thirty-fifth from the top.

"I'm sorry, Gloria, but I have to ask you to do a bit of work. Would you please deal the deck into four piles, alternately."

She deals out the cards as requested (Illus. 30). Each pile contains 13 cards.

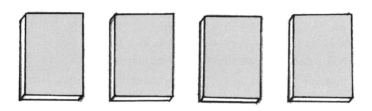

ILLUS. 30

You apparently fall into a trance—your eyes are almost shut and your voice is fainter and almost a monotone. "I think I hear the voice of Madam Flaboda. She has volunteered to help me with this effect. "What do you want, Madam Flaboda?" Pause. "Madam Flaboda tells me that you should pick up this pile ..." Indicate the third pile that was dealt out. "... and deal it into three piles, just as you dealt before."

You pick up the other three piles and set them aside.

Gloria does as requested. There are now three piles; the first pile contains five cards, the other two contain four cards each (Illus. 31).

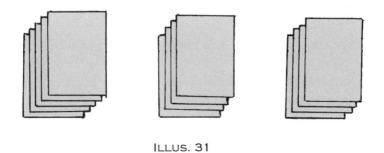

ILLUS. 31

"What next, Madam Flaboda?" Apparently the Madam speaks to you for a few moments. Indicate the middle pile of the three. "Madam Flaboda tells me that you should pick up this pile and deal it into two piles."

Pick up the other two piles and set them aside with the other discards.

Again Gloria follows Madam Flaboda's directions. There are now two piles, each containing two cards.

Listen to Madam Flaboda again. "Gloria, the Madam wants you to pick up this pile and deal it into two piles." Indicate the *first* pile she dealt to.

Pick up the other pile and place it with the other discards.

Gloria deals out the two cards separately. Listen again to Madam Flaboda. Point to the first card Gloria dealt. "The Madam says that *this* is your chosen card."

Set the other card with the discards.

"Please turn the card over."

Unbelievable! Madam Flaboda is right.

Review

1) Gloria looks at the top card of the 18-card pile and places the other two piles on top of it.

2) She deals the entire deck into four piles.

3) She deals the *third* pile into three piles. (The other cards are set aside.)

4) She deals the middle pile into two piles. (The other cards are set aside.)

5) She deals the first pile into two piles. (The other cards are set aside.)

6) Two cards are on the table. Point to the first card, saying, "The Madam says that *this* is your chosen card."

Note

As I promised, here is another way to begin the trick. After Gloria shuffles the cards, say, "Gloria, I'd like you to just pile up some cards, like this."

The cards are face up, so you fan out three face-up cards and drop them face up onto the table. Fan out four face-up cards, and toss them face up on top of the first group. Make sure the cards are not in a neat pile but form a rather sloppy group. Do the same with five more cards, and then with six. So into a face-up group you've tossed three cards, four cards, five cards, and six cards—18 in all. Straighten your pile a bit.

Hand the face-up deck to Gloria. Indicate a space in front

of her on the table. She deals out a pile of cards, several at a time, just as you did. She should have some face-up cards left.

Take them from her and place them face down onto the table. Straighten up your pile and put it face down next to the ones you just set down. Finally, take her pile, straighten it, and place it face down next to the other two.

You now complete the trick exactly as described above. First, you force Gloria to choose the 18-card pile. Then you have her perform the various deals.

THESE ARE GOLD

Professor Hoffmann (Angelo John Lewis), a 19th-century magician, wrote three exhaustive books on magic. In one of them, *Modern Magic*, he explained this trick. It's hard to believe that a trick that's more than 100 years old can still fool people, but I have performed it successfully many times. I have modernized it slightly, tossed in a touch of my own, and thrown in few patter points.

Explain to the group: "I believe many of you are familiar with a trick in which three columns of seven cards are dealt out. The spectator thinks of his card and tells the magician which column his card is in. The magician gathers up the cards and then deals them out again in three columns. Again the spectator tells him which column, and again the magician deals the cards into three columns. In fact, the magician does this three times in all. Finally, the magician tells the spectator the name of his card.

"I intend to do better than that. Jennifer, will you help me." She will. "I'm going to deal out as many columns of cards as you want, Jennifer—five columns of five cards each, six columns of six cards each, or seven columns of seven cards each. Which would you like?"

She makes her choice.

Let's suppose that she chooses six columns of six cards each. You deal out six cards face up in a row. Starting at the left you next deal a face-up card on top of each of the original six, all cards overlapping so that spectators can see the indices of the first six. In Illus. 32, you can see the first card covered appropriately. Continue in this way until all remaining 36 cards have been dealt out face up.

Ask Gary to also assist you. "Jennifer, I'd like you and Gary to each mentally choose a card. It would be better if you don't both choose the same card, so I'll turn my back while you point out your choices to one another."

Turn your back. When you face the group once more, say, "The trick I just explained to you deals with threes—three columns, three choices. My attempt at mind reading deals with twos. Two persons choose a card, and two times I'm told in which columns the cards lie.

"Jennifer, in which column is your card?"

She points it out. You note the top card of that column and commit it to memory. Do I mean that you have to actually remember the name of this card? Yes, I do. And another one besides. Hold it! I'll explain how easy it is. Let's suppose that the top card in that row is the queen of spades. Say to yourself, "Queen of spades, queen of spades, queen of spades, queen of spades." And every time you have a few seconds, repeat, "Queen of spades, queen of spades."

Turn to Gary. "Which column is your card in, Gary?" He tells you. Note the top card of that column. Suppose that the top card in that column is the 7 of clubs. Say to yourself, "Queen of spades, 7 of clubs. Queen of spades, 7 of clubs. Queen of spades, 7 of clubs." And when you pause in your delivery, repeat the names again.

You, yourself, must close up each row of cards, because you can't explain in a short time precisely how this should be done. All you do, really, is push each column up from the bottom (Illus. 33). The cards remain precisely in the same order.

You make this generous offer: "Jennifer, please gather up the piles, one on top of the other. You can gather them up in any order you wish."

Big deal! If it mattered, you'd have never made the offer.

Guess what you're doing mentally as she's gathering up the piles. That's right. You're saying, over and over, "Queen of spades, 7 of clubs." Or the names of whatever cards you're supposed to be remembering.

ILLUS. 33

YOUR HAND SLIDES THE CARDS UPWARD.

Take the collected piles from Jennifer and turn the combined pile face down. Deal the cards face up precisely as you did at the beginning, ending up with six columns of cards. (And while you're dealing, what are you saying mentally? That's right. You're repeating the names of your key cards.)

Ask Jennifer, "Which column is your card in?" She tells you. Your job now is to find the card which you remembered as the top card of the pile Jennifer originally selected. So you look around until you find the queen of spades. Note the position that it is from the top of its column. Let's suppose that it is third from the top. Note the card that is third from the top of the pile Jennifer just pointed out. That's her card. (You can count this out either from the top or the bottom—and I hate to insult your intelligence, but I have a lot of time on my hands—you must count from the same place with both piles.) Pick out her card and hand it to her.

Do exactly the same thing with Gary. He tells you which column his card is in. You find your original key card for Gary—in our example, the 7 of clubs. Note its position from the top. His card is in the same position in the column he pointed out. Pick it out and hand it to him.

The trick has a powerful effect. Someday you may just be able to do it with three spectators.

Note

Occasionally, the two spectators will initially choose a card from the same pile. Nothing changes except that you must remember only one card—the one at the top of the pile which contains both cards.

You Need All 52

That's right. The trick will probably work if you have fewer than 52 cards, but to be on the safe side, use a complete deck.

Once more I'm indebted to my good friend Wally Wilson for this fascinating trick. As always, I've made a few adjustments, and have made it nearly 100 percent perfect by offering a few "outs" in case you have a stubborn spectator.

Maria seems to think she's psychic, so let's give her an opportunity to display her technique.

"Please shuffle the cards, Maria. And then cut the deck into three piles, approximately even. You can move cards around to make sure the piles are fairly even."

Turn your back and add, "Please pick up one of the piles. Turn them so the faces are toward yourself. Fan the cards out so that you can see the faces. Now think of a card somewhere near the center of the group."

Pause.

"Now close up the cards. Place that pile on top of one of the piles on the table. Place the other pile on top of all."

Pick up the deck and begin an overhand shuffle, running off several cards. Stop suddenly, saying, "Wait! I'll mix them up in a much better way."

Place the cards in your right hand below the cards you shuffled off. Thus, all you've done really is mix up the top dozen cards or so. (If you find this part is too difficult, just eliminate it.)

You now mix the cards like this:

1) Deal off, singly, three cards, placing them in a row on the table.

2) Fan off two cards and place them on top of the first card. Do the same for the other two.

3) Fan off three cards and place them on top of the first group. Do the same for the other two.

4) Fan off two cards and place them on top of the first group. Do the same for the other two.

5) Deal off, singly, three cards, placing them on top of each pile. Say, "Let's start all over again."

6) Deal off, singly, three cards, placing one on top of each pile.

7) Fan off two cards and place them on top of the first group. Do the same for the other two.

8) Fan off three cards and place them on top of the first group. Do the same for the other two.

9) Fan off two cards and place them on top of the first group. Do the same for the other two.

You have one card remaining. Place it on the bottom of the middle pile.

It's easy enough to remember:

1 2 3 2 1 (Let's start all over again) 1 2 3 2 (1 card left)

Even up the packets. "Now let's see how psychic you are, Maria. Which packet do you think your card is in?"

She chooses one. "See if your card is there, Maria." Turn your head away and fan though the cards face up.

If it's there, congratulate her on her magnificent powers. If not, ask her to choose one of the two remaining piles. Again, turn your head away and fan through the cards face up. If it is, tell her, "Not bad, Maria. Not perfect, but not bad."

If it's not there, tell her, "Maria, congratulations. You have 100 percent perfect negative psychic power."

In any event, collect the cards, placing on top the pile that contains the chosen card.

"Maria, I believe that we can find your card. What's the name of the card?"

She tells you. Let's suppose that it's the king of spades. "Good. Now what we must do is test your faith. We'll find out if you believe me. Let's spell it."

The selected card can be in any of four positions in the pile and you will spell to it. The card can be in the sixth, seventh, eighth, or ninth position from the top. Here's how you do it.

Deal the cards into a face-up pile, placing down one card for each letter in the spelling of the word BELIEVE. If the king of spades comes up as you deal the last E, stop, saying, "You do believe, Maria." If it does not, turn over the next card. If it's the king of spades, make the remark to Maria. If it's not, immediately continue by spelling the word ME. Say the letter M for the card you just turned up.

Turn over the next card, saying E. If that's the king of spades, say, "Believe me, Maria, you have faith in me."

If not, the next card should be the king of spades. Turn it over, making the comment to Maria.

Suppose the spectator is a real chowderhead and that the chosen card is not one of the four cards. Look through the pile until you find the card and cut it to the top, all the while declaring how disappointed you are.

You now have the card on top. Say, "Let's try something different." Proceed to force the card on Maria, using one of the four forces at the beginning of "Mental Tricks," from pages 27 to 38.

When Maria chooses the card, say, "What did you select?" She names the card. "Oh, sure," you say, still miffed. "Now it shows up."

Note

You have just finished reading my so-called surefire version of Wally's trick. Wally, however, assures me that his version hardly ever fails. He suggests that you take the pile in which the spectator's card lies and say, "To locate your card, we must use the mystic expression, 'I believe.'"

You then spell out I BELIEVE, and the selection should appear on either the last card of the spelling or the next card.

Wally assures us that we don't have to worry too much about saving the trick: "I have found by experimenting over and over that the thought-of card will end up in the eighth or ninth position after the shuffle. Rarely will it be the seventh or tenth. The odds are so great in your favor, it is a worthy effect, I have found. Try it and see for yourself. What makes it work is the subtle suggestion, 'Think of a card, somewhere near the middle of the fan.'"

If the card is not in the eighth or ninth position, you can always resort to the forcing method I described earlier.

TAKE YOUR Q

Ed Marlo, master card-trick performer and inventor, occasionally would develop a trick that was far more complicated than it needed to be. Case in point is this variation of an old favorite, familiarly known as "The Q Trick." Marlo, for some unfathomable reason, felt there had to be a memorized setup. Actually, an easy variation can be performed with a bit of subtlety, as I will explain.

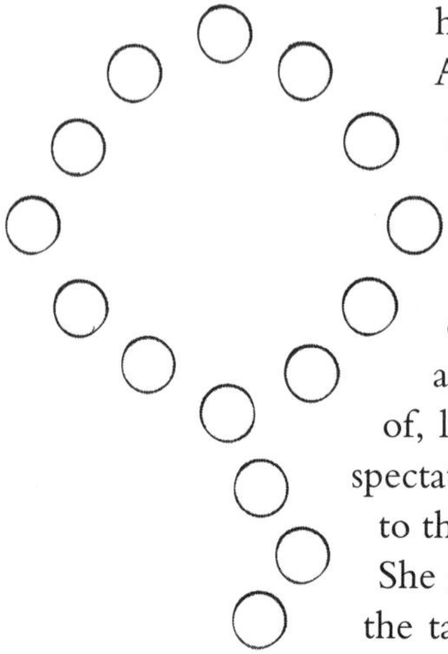

The original basic trick is this: A number of objects— coins, for instance—are placed in a circle. A tail is added, consisting of, let's say, three coins (Illus. 34). A spectator—Melissa, for instance—is told to think of a number from five to ten. She is told, "Starting at the bottom of the tail, please count your number up the tail and around the circle to the left. Then, starting with the coin you landed on, count the same number back around the circle to the right. But don't go down the tail—just stay on the circle."

You turn away while Melissa does this. Regardless, when you turn back, you know exactly which coin she landed on. How? There are three coins in the tail. In Illus. 35, X marks the coin in the circle to which the tail is attached. Start with the coin to the right of this coin and continue counting counterclockwise to the exact number of coins in the tail—in this instance, three. The last coin you count is the one chosen. In the illustration, this is marked with a Y.

ILLUS. 35

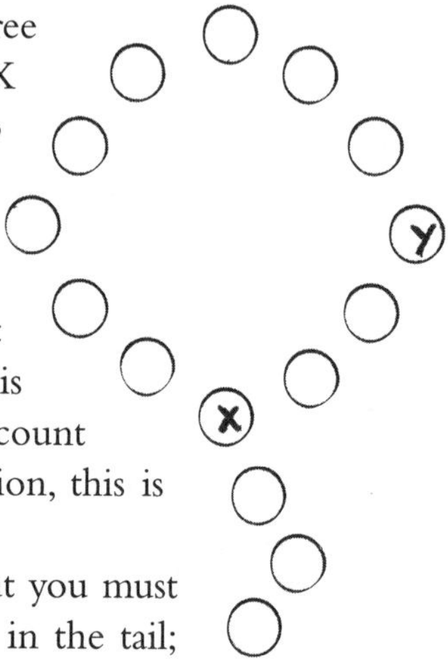

The trick may be repeated, but you must slyly change the number of coins in the tail;

otherwise, Melissa will end up on the same number.

Marlo's version is done with playing cards. He decided to form a Q of face-up cards and then have two cards chosen as described: the one the spectator lands on first, and the one the spectator lands on after counting back. Both cards are revealed.

This can be done by using an elimination process, but here is a much easier trick that seems to accomplish the same thing.

We might as well have Melissa help out. Ask her to shuffle the deck. When she finishes, say to her, "Please deal out 12 cards face up in the form of a clock." She does. The result should resemble Illus. 36, except that the cards would be face up.

Take the remainder of the deck from her, saying, "Now we'll add a little tail."

Place a two-card tail on the circle, connecting them at the card that would represent six if the layout were a clock (Illus. 37).

"Here's what we'll do, Melissa. We'll have you choose a card. You'll think of a

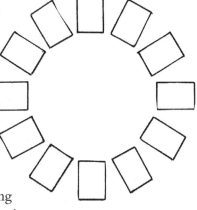

**THE CARDS ARE
ACTUALLY FACE UP**

ILLUS. 37

number from five to ten. Let's say you think of six. You count up the tail like this."

You demonstrate by counting up the tail and then to the left, stopping at the card at the count of six. "Then you start on the card you land on and count back the same number, going to your right. But don't go down the tail; just keep going around the circle. The card you land on will be your choice."

Show the direction of the count back, but don't actually perform it.

Turn away while Melissa performs her duties. Turn back and, after concentrating, divine the name of her choice. As with the coins, you simply start counting with the card to the right of the card to which the tail is attached. And you count counter-clockwise to the same number of cards as are in the tail—in this instance, two. The last card you count is the one chosen.

"Now let's try for two cards," you say. "To make it even more difficult, let's make the tail a bit longer."

Add two cards to the tail.

Carefully explain: "Again I'd like you to think of a number from five to ten. You can even choose the same number if you wish—anything to fool me. Follow the same procedure as before—counting up this side …" Indicate counting up and going to the left. "… and, starting on the card you land on, counting the same number back this way." Indicate the counter-clockwise direction.

"The card you land on will be your choice, just as before. But then I'd like you to choose a second card. And I want you to use a lucky number for that. What would be a good lucky number?"

If Melissa should say any number other than seven, say, "That is a good lucky number, but I think a better one would be seven. So start on your first choice and count off seven cards, going either way. The card you land on will be your second choice."

Make sure she understands the directions; then turn away.

When you turn back, you again concentrate fiercely and eventually name both cards. You count to the first card by counting four cards counterclockwise, starting with the card to the right of the one to which the tail is attached. The second card? Oh, you've already figured that out. It's seven cards away from the first choice, no matter which direction you count.

Note

You do not immediately do a two-card revelation, because you want Melissa to become familiar with the basic procedure first. It's possible that she might become confused if she must choose two cards to begin with.

LET'S LOSE YOUR CARD

An extremely observant spectator would be able to perform this trick after watching it once, but fortunately there is sufficient folderol to cause confusion. The spectator would have to recall how the cards are cut, the exact sentence you use, and the precise procedure at the end.

Charles is seldom surprised by anything, so it's time you caused his eyes to widen somewhat. Hand him the deck and ask him to give it a good shuffle. Continue with appropriate pauses:

"Set the deck down, Charles, and then divide it in half. It doesn't have to be exact—just about in half."

"Push one half of the deck aside and cut the remaining cards in half—again, just about half."

"Push one of those piles aside."

"Charles, please pick up the remaining pile and give it a shuffle."

"I'll turn my head while you take a look at the bottom card of the pile. And show it to the rest of the group, please."

"Now let's lose your card. Spell out, 'Let's lose your card,' transferring one card to the bottom for each letter in the spelling."

Make sure he understands what to do and that he does it properly.

"Let's mix them further. Please deal the top card onto the table, and move the next card to the bottom. Deal the next card on top of the first card, and move the next card to the bottom. Please continue until all the cards are in a pile on the table."

Then say, "For the first time, I'll touch the cards."

ILLUS. 38

Show that both your hands are empty. Pick up the pile and straighten it out. Hold it in your left hand in the dealer's grip.

"What's the name of your card, Charles?"

He names it.

"Watch."

Place your right hand over the deck, completely concealing it (Illus. 38). Give your hands a little up-and-down shake.

"And here it is." Turn over the top card of the packet.

Notes

1) It's hard to believe that this trick actually works. But as you'll discover, it does, and most entertainingly. Why all the cutting? For one thing, the trick would be much too cumbersome with a full deck. For another thing, the trick only works if there are eight to 16 cards. The cutting makes sure that the number of cards is right.

2) Why do we always have the spectator show the card to others? Hard to believe, but once in a while a spectator will actually lie about his chosen card just to goof you up. So it doesn't hurt to take out a little insurance that this won't happen.

3) If you are skilled at performing an overhand shuffle, you might try this when you take the packet from the spectator: Shuffle the top card to the bottom of the packet, and then shuffle it back to the top. Now reveal the chosen card.

EASY SPELLER

To perform this excellent spelling trick, you must be familiar with "Simplicity Itself," a method of locating a chosen card (see page 11). As described, you have arranged to have your key card just above the chosen card.

Let's suppose that Nancy has chosen a card and that you know the card above it in the deck. Say to her, "I want you to be sure that your card has not been removed from the deck. Watch for it, please, but don't say anything when we come to it."

Fan through the deck until you come to the chosen card (on the near side of the key card, of course). Notice the value and suit of the chosen card. Let's suppose that it is the 9 of clubs. Starting with the chosen card, proceed to spell it out: pass one card to the right-hand pile for each letter in the spelling.

Note the suit and value of the next card.

You can now forget about the chosen card. Let's suppose that the next card is the queen of spades. Spell this out mentally as you fan through the cards, in the same way as you did with the chosen card.

Cut the cards so that the last card in the spelling goes to the top.

Everyone is now observing the new bottom card. Proudly announce, "I think I can say with authority that this is not your chosen card, right?"

Of course you're right.

"Let's see if we can locate your card by spelling it out. Suppose your card were the queen of spades." Name the second card you spelled out. Make it casual, as though you're naming a card at random. Spell out the queen of spades, dealing one card into a pile onto the table for each letter. Turn over the last letter of the spelling.

"There it is—the queen of spades."

Hand Nancy the deck. "What was the name of your card, Nancy?" She names it. Have her spell it out. When she turns over the last card of the spelling, she, along with everyone else, will be quite surprised.

General Tricks

I could discover no other category for these tricks—which means they are unique. Perhaps these are the most interesting tricks in the book.

Point with Pride

Required here is a modest amount of nimbleness. I recommend that you at least give this a try; it has a powerful effect on viewers.

It's essential that the deck be shuffled, so you might as well call on Sal, who fancies himself an expert with the pasteboards.

Take the deck back, saying, "I've acquired a certain amount of skill with this finger." Hold up the first finger of your left hand. "Sometimes I can rub this finger on the back of a card and tell what it is." Pause. "And, of course, sometimes I can't. Let's try it out."

Hold the deck in the dealing position in your left hand. With your right hand, cut off a small packet of cards and set

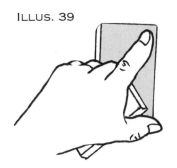

ILLUS. 39

it on the table. Still holding the deck, extend the first finger of your left hand. Rub the tip of the finger against the top card of the packet on the table, preferably in the upper right corner (Illus. 39).

As you rub the card, the left fingers have pushed over the top card of those in your left hand so that you can see the value and suit (Illus. 40). After you have seen the card, push it even with the others. Do this while stopping the rubbing movement and turning the hand back to its normal position.

Shake your head. "I can't seem to get that one. Let's try another."

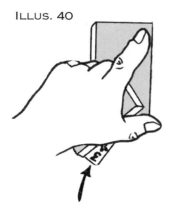

PEEK AT THIS CARD.

With your right hand, cut off a small pile from the cards you're holding and place it on top of the pile on the table. Naturally, you know the top card of those on the table.

Perform the rubbing procedure again. As you do, name the card. At the same time, push the next card over for a peek. Return the left hand to its normal position. "Let's see how I did." With your right hand, turn over the top card of the packet on the table. "I can't believe it; I got it absolutely right. Let's try again." Turn the card face down.

Cut off another small packet and place it on top of the pile on the table. Rub the top card of the packet. This time, however, do not peek at the top card of those in your left hand. Move your left hand away from the tabled cards. "I can't seem to get it."

Transfer the remainder of the deck to your right hand. Presumably, these cards are interfering with your rubbing ability. Rub the top card of the tabled cards again. Gradually name the card. For instance, you might say, "I think I'm getting the suit. It's a 6. No, I'm confused because the cards are reversed; it's a 9." You could equally well confuse a 5 and a 2, a 3 and an 8, an ace and a 4, or any two face cards.

Give the cards another rub and reveal the suit. The idea is to stress that it's not easy, and that you're not perfect.

Turn over the top card of the packet, showing that once more you are correct. It's quite enough to detect two cards; no need to go further. If the group insists, you might say, "No, I was pretty lucky to get two out of three. I'd better not try again."

If, however, you feel confident in your ability to peek, you might proceed. Fail on the next card while taking another peek. Then, with great difficulty, detect the card after that.

As with the revelation of the second card, first rub with the deck in your left hand. Run into difficulty. Transfer the deck to the right hand to make the rubbing easier. After considerable tribulation, name the card.

Under no circumstances do the trick more than three times.

CRIME DOES NOT PAY

This idea is another Wally Wilson invention. The principle is used in a number of tricks, but the actual working here is unique.

Spread the cards from left hand to right, counting off 15. Hand the packet to Janet, asking her to shuffle them. Count off another 15, handing the packet to Ron, also requesting a shuffle. (Incidentally, as you count off the 15, don't make it clear that you're counting. You might do well to pass the cards three at a time to help conceal the process.)

Have Janet and Ron set their packets face down onto the table.

"Now I'd like you both to cut off a pile from your packet and set the pile down right next to your packet."

Make sure that the two sets of packets are fairly widely separated (Illus. 41). This is so that future directions will not be misunderstood.

ILLUS. 41

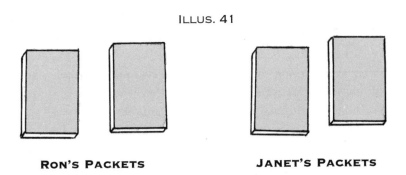

RON'S PACKETS   **JANET'S PACKETS**

Have both Janet and Ron choose a card from the rest of the deck. The cards are turned face up so that all can see them. (The rest of the deck is set aside and will not be used for the rest of the trick.)

"One of those cards will be a detective, and one will be a criminal. I don't like to hurt your feelings, Ron, but I think you'll make a better criminal. Janet, you'll be the detective."

"Janet, please place your card face up onto either one of your packets."

She does.

"Ron, pick up either one of your packets and put it right on top of Janet's card."

He does.

"Now, Ron, put your card—the criminal—face down onto your packet. We need him face down so that he'll be harder to find."

He does.

Point to the packet that does not contain Janet's selected card. "Janet, please put this pile on top of Ron's pile."

She does. Instruct Janet to place either pile on top of the other one.

Both Ron and Janet give the entire packet a complete cut. If they desire, the packet may be cut again.

"Which of you wants to be the big dealer?"

Let's suppose that Ron volunteers. Have him deal the cards alternately into two piles.

"Obviously, we have to keep the packet with the detective."

Set the other packet aside.

The remaining cards are dealt into two piles. The pile containing the detective is retained; the other is set aside.

This is continued until only two cards are left.

"We have tried our best to confuse the detective. Let's see if she was able to overcome the odds and capture the criminal."

Turn over the face-down card. It's the criminal.

Review

1) Ron and Janet each receive 15 cards.
2) Both divide their cards into two piles.
3) Each chooses a card from the remaining deck.
4) Janet's card is the detective and is placed face up on top of one of her packets.
5) Ron places one of his packets on top of Janet's card.
6) Ron's card is the criminal. It's placed face down on top of his remaining packet.
7) You point to the packet that does not contain Janet's card and tell her to place this packet on top of Ron's packet.
8) Janet is told to combine the packets, placing either one on top.
9) The combined packet is given several complete cuts.
10) One of your assistants deals the combined packet alternately into two piles. The pile containing the face-up card is kept, while the others are set aside. The deal is repeated until only two cards remain. Turning over Ron's selected card, you declare that the great detective has found the criminal.

B'Gosh

A good magician learns early on that the most important part of a trick is the effect. Yes, the presentation should be entertaining, and the magician should have a pleasing personality, but if the result is mediocre, everything else is a waste of time. Good magicians will tell you that if you need a special card to make a trick work, that's just fine. Or, if the deck must be secretly set up in advance to perform a super-miracle, that's delightful. And, if a spectator is a confederate (or plant) and the result is remarkable, that's absolutely perfect.

Such is the case with this trick, which Martin Gardner credits to Chris Schoke.

Let's suppose that your secret helper is Grace. Tell the group that you'll need two volunteers. Naturally, Grace raises her hand and is chosen. Of the half-dozen other eager helpers, you pick Arnold.

Hand the deck to Arnold and ask him to shuffle the cards. He does.

"Arnold, please give the deck to Grace, who will also give the deck a good shuffle."

Grace shuffles the deck thoroughly. But at the end, she casually glances at the bottom card and then sets the deck face down onto the table. Let's say that the bottom card is the 6 of clubs. Grace will remember this card. Later on, she will pretend that this is the card that she has chosen.

"Arnold, please cut off about half the cards and set them in front of you."

He does.

"Now, Arnold, you can take the top card of either pile and look at it. Don't let anyone else see it, please."

He does what you ask.

"Grace, I'd like you to choose a card from the top of either pile. Look at it, but don't let anyone else see it."

Grace takes a card, all right, but the card she remembers is the 6 of clubs that was on the bottom of the deck.

"Arnold, please put your card back on top of either pile. And Grace, put your card back on top of the other pile." Pause. "Now on top of either pile is a chosen card. Grace, I'd like you to put the two piles together and then give them a cut, or give each pile a cut and then put them together—your choice."

On the bottom of one pile is the 6 of clubs that Grace sneaked a peek at. If Arnold's card is on top of this pile, Grace gives the pile a complete cut—that is, she takes off a portion from the top, sets it onto the table, and then puts the balance of that pile on top of the pile she just placed on the table.

She gives the other pile a complete cut. Then she puts one of the piles on top of the other. The upshot is that the 6 of clubs is now on top of the card that Arnold selected.

Suppose that on the bottom of the first pile is the 6 of clubs and that Arnold's chosen card is on top of the second pile. Grace places the first pile on top of the second pile. This puts the 6 of clubs on top of Arnold's chosen card. Then she gives the entire deck a complete cut. Little known to the general public is that a complete cut does not change the basic order of the cards; regardless of the number of complete cuts, the cards remain in the same relative order. Therefore, Grace may cut the cards again. And Arnold should give the deck a few complete cuts as well.

Pick up the deck. Give the cards a snap, or riffle the ends. You can do the latter by putting your fingers at the outer end and your thumb at the inner end. Bend the cards upward (Illus. 42); let them fall quickly. The whole idea is to do something that could pass for a clever move. You don't want the group to think that the trick is automatic, or—heaven forbid—that one of the participants assisted you.

Address Grace and Arnold: "I'm going to deal the cards out face up. If either of you sees your card, tell me immediately."

From the face-down deck, slowly deal the cards into a face-up pile. Eventually, Grace will see the card she glimpsed on the bottom of the deck, the 6 of clubs. The minute she does, she says, "Stop! That's my card."

"Fair enough. Grace, your card and Arnold's card were separated in the deck. And the deck was given several cuts. The only thing I did was give the deck a magical snap. Let's see what happened." Deal the next card face down in front of Arnold.

"What was your chosen card, Arnold?"

He names it.

Turn it over, showing that the two chosen cards have somehow joined together in the deck.

Thank the two for their assistance and move on to your next trick.

THE TEN TRICK

Once more I'm indebted to my good friend Wally Wilson, who showed me this extraordinary stunt many years ago. I have no idea who invented it; I do know that I have added a few wrinkles that I think enhance it.

You really should try this out on your friends; it may well be the most impressive trick in this book.

Hand the deck to Sally and ask her to give it a good shuffle. When she finishes, continue, "Now please pick out any three cards and set them face down over here." Indicate a spot on the

ILLUS. 43

THE CARDS ARE ACTUALLY FACE UP.

table well out of the way. "You may look at the three cards or not, whatever you wish."

When she's ready say, "Please deal four rows of cards face up. Each row should consist of five cards. Put the rows one below the other."

The rows should look like Illus. 43, except that the cards would be face up.

Take the deck back from Sally.

"I'm going to go through all the cards in the deck, trying to check out all 13 values. I'll go through the cards only once, and then I'll try to tell you the value of each one of your chosen cards."

All of that is baloney, of course. You'll go through the deck, all right, but you'll do it in such a way that you'll know absolutely what the three cards are.

Look over the 20 face-up cards. You're seeking a pair that adds up to ten—5 and 5, 6 and 4, 7 and 3, 8 and 2, or 9 and 1 (1 is an ace).

Take off the top card of the deck and turn it face up; place this card face up on one card of the pair you've discovered—a 6, for instance. Take off the next card, turn it face up, and place it onto a 4. Since 6 and 4 add up to 10, you've correctly covered your first pair. Naturally, you've now added two new face-up cards. Look for another pair that adds up to 10 and cover each of the cards with a face-up card from the deck.

There is only one other combination that you cover. See if a combination of these three values is showing: king, queen, jack. If so, cover each one with a face-up card.

How about tens? You don't cover tens; you just let them be.

Continue covering pairs that add up to 10 and king-queen-jack combinations until you hold no more cards. Look over all the face-up cards. How many tens are showing? Let's suppose that four tens are showing; obviously, 10 is not one of the chosen cards. If, however, there are three tens showing, then one of the chosen cards is a 10. If two tens are showing, Sally has chosen two tens. And in the extremely unlikely event that one 10 is showing, goofy old Sally has selected three tens. If Sally has chosen any tens tell her about it at the end of the trick, not now.

You now pick up all the cards on the table, based on the top face-up card of each pile. You pick up each pair that adds up to 10, each king-queen-jack combination, and each pile topped by a 10. Each pile is picked up by your right hand and placed face up into your left hand.

(Sometimes, before picking up the cards, you'll be holding one card that could not be dealt out. What do you do? For your first pick-up from the table, select a stack on which the top face-up card will add up to 10 with the card you're holding. If you're holding a face card, pick up the two piles that complete the king-queen-jack combination.)

At the end, there will be some cards left on the table—these cards do not get picked up, because they do not fulfill the requirements. Let's say that the cards are a 3, a 6, and an 8. You subtract each from 10. This gives you the values of the three selected cards. Three subtracted from 10 gives you 7. Six subtracted from 10 give you 4. Eight subtracted from 10 gives you 2.

As you gather up the last cards, remember the values 7, 4, and 2. Tell Sally, "I can't tell you the suits of your cards, but I know their values. You selected a 7, a 4, and a 2." Repeat yourself to make sure it's clear. Sally turns over her cards to reveal that you're correct.

Suppose that the cards remaining include two face cards— a king and a queen, for instance. The card missing from the king-queen-jack combination is the jack. So one of Sally's selections was a jack. Clearly, whatever value is missing from the combination is held by Sally. If at the end you have a spot card and one face card, you subtract the value of the spot card from 10 to determine one of the chosen cards. The other two are cards that complete the king-queen-jack combination. If the card is a queen, for instance, Sally holds both the king and the jack.

Oh-oh! Big trouble. After the pickup, only one card remains on the table. This means that Sally holds two cards that add up to 10. After all this work, are you defeated? Of course not.

Let's suppose that the only card left on the table is an ace. You know that one of the cards held by Sally is a 9 (10 - 1 = 9). You say, "Sally, I'm having big trouble today. I know absolutely that one of your cards is an ace, right?"

She looks at her cards. You're right.

"I just can't get the other two. I have sort of an idea. Maybe I can work it out if you tell me one of the other two cards."

Oh, you sly little rapscallion. When she tells you the value of one of the cards, you subtract that value from 10, which gives you the value of the other card.

Let's say that Sally tells you that one of the cards is a 6. "Six?" you say, looking quite puzzled. Murmur, "What can the other one be?" Ponder a moment. "Oh, of course. The other card is a 4."

Right you are.

There's no reason why you can't perform the trick again. Believe me, no one will catch on to how you determine what cards to cover.

FOUR OF A KIND

PILES OF ACES

Years ago, William Simon came up with this excellent four-ace trick. As with most tricks, a great deal of its effectiveness depends on the proper presentation.

A bit of preparation is necessary. You need two aces on top of the deck, and two aces together somewhere in the middle.

To start, get the aid of two assistants. Humphrey and Adele are always hanging around together, so they would be perfect.

Fan through the face-up deck so that all can see, saying, "As you'll notice, it's a regular deck of cards."

Raise the cards toward you as you near the middle. Watch for the two aces in the middle. Make them the last two cards that you pass into the right hand. Separate the cards at this point (Illus. 44). You should be holding a face-up pile in each hand. On the bottom of each face-up pile are two face-up aces. Illus. 45 shows the position of both sets of aces. The aces are not actually fanned out. Even the cards up and lower your hands.

Set the two piles face up onto the table.

Point to the pile nearest Adele. Say to her, "Adele, I'd like you to cut some cards off this pile and hand them to me."

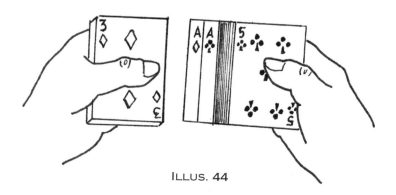

ILLUS. 44

ILLUS. 45

She does.

"Humphrey, please cut some cards off the other pile and hand them to me."

After you receive the cards, form them into a single pile and set them aside.

"It would seem that each of you started with a different number of cards. And then each of you undoubtedly cut off a different number of cards."

Pick up Humphrey's pile, turn it face down, and hand it to him. Hand Adele her pile, also face down. (If Humphrey and Adele were to pick up the piles, there might be an accidental revelation of the aces.)

"Please, each of you deal your cards into a face-down pile."

After each has dealt out several cards, say, "Each of you can stop whenever you want. But please don't stop at exactly the same time."

They stop dealing. Take the cards they're still holding and set them aside with the other discards.

"Now, Humphrey, I'd like you to pick up your pile and then deal your cards into two piles, alternating—first one card on the left, then one on the right. Continue until all your cards are dealt out."

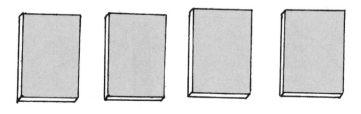

ILLUS. 46

When he's done, direct Adele to do the same thing. Finally Adele finishes. Line up the piles as in Illus. 46.

"I hope everyone noticed that Humphrey and Adele each cut off a different number of cards. Then they dealt out as many cards as they wanted. And again, each chose a different number. So, of course, we have considerable variation between the two sets of piles. Despite all these differences, I'm sure that Humphrey and Adele have a certain compatibility, a mysterious mutuality. Let's see if I'm right."

Turn over the top cards of the four piles, revealing the four aces. Let everyone have a look for several seconds.

ACES BY THE NUMBER

Frank Garcia applied an old principle to a four-ace trick. I've spruced it up a bit to simplify the trick and eliminate a sleight.

Before starting, you must have the four aces on top. Later, you will secretly move 15 cards on top of them. If you want to make this your first trick, put the four aces on top; then count 15 cards from the bottom of the deck and place them on top of the aces. You're ready to go.

Or you can try it this way: Start your performance with the four aces on top of the deck. Perform a few tricks that will keep them there. Or perform a few tricks that will keep them together somewhere in the deck. When you're ready, without explanation casually fan through the deck and cut the aces to the top. Chat with the group for a minute or two. Now you're ready to add 15 cards to the top.

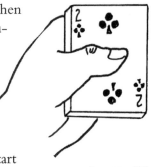

ILLUS. 47

Turn the deck face up so that all can see the bottom card (Illus. 47). Start fanning through the deck, saying, "The cards seem to be well mixed."

Count off eight cards as you fan through the deck. Place these eight cards to the back (top) of the deck. Count off seven more cards and also place these on top of the deck. Spread out several more cards, saying, "I think you'll agree." Close up the cards and turn the deck face down.

You now have 15 cards on top, followed by the four aces.

I don't see where Donna has any right to sit there like a lump, while you're working your head off; she should be willing to assist you.

"Donna, please name a number between 15 and 20." The word "between" confines her choice to four numbers: 16, 17, 18, and 19. This is important, as you'll see.

Let's say that Donna names 18. Fan out the cards at the top of the deck. Let everyone see that you're taking five cards. Take the five cards into your right hand and set them face down onto the table, saying, "Five."

Do it again, taking another five cards and setting them to the right of the first group. Say, "Ten."

Repeat, saying, "15." This pile goes to the right of all the others.

Fan off three more cards, saying, "And three is 18." Place these to the right of the other three piles. (If Donna had chosen 16, you would place one card here. If she had chosen 17, you would place two cards here. And, of course, if she had chosen 19, you would place four cards here.)

Point to the pile on the left, saying, "Five."

Place the cards you're holding on top of this pile.

Touch the next pile to the right, saying, "Ten." Touch the next pile to the right, saying, "15." Touch the three-card pile, saying, "And three is 18."

Take the top card of this pile and place it, face down, in front of the other piles (Illus. 48). This card is an ace.

Pick up the remaining cards in this pile and place them on top of the deck, which is resting on top of the first pile you placed down. (Where the chosen number is 16, there will be no cards left, which works out fine.)

Place the other two piles onto the deck in any order. Pick up the deck.

"More work, Donna. Please name a number between ten and 15."

Let's say that she names 12.

As before, you place down five cards, saying, "Five." Then

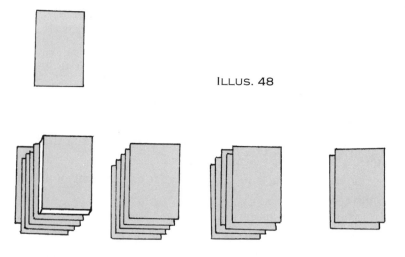

ILLUS. 48

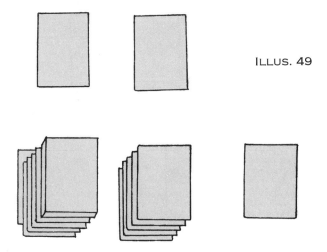

place down five more to the right of this pile, saying, "Ten." Place two cards to the right of all, saying, "And two is 12."

Point to the pile on the left, repeating, "Five." Place the rest of the deck on top of this pile. Point to the next pile to the right, saying, "Ten." Point to the two-card pile, saying, "And two is 12."

Remove the top card of this last pile and place it, face down, to the right of the first ace you've set down (Illus. 49).

Place the remaining card (or cards) in this pile onto the deck, which rests on top of the first pile you set down. (If Donna chose 11, no cards will remain in this last pile—which is all right.)

Place the five-card pile on top of the deck.

"Once more, Donna. This time, please name a number between five and ten."

Suppose she says nine. Fan out five cards and place them onto the table, saying, "Five." Fan out four cards and, placing them to the right of the first pile, say, "And four is nine."

Touch the first pile, saying, "Five."

This time do not place the deck onto the five-card pile.

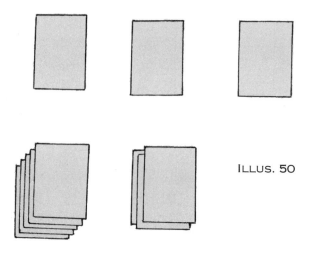

ILLUS. 50

Simply point to the four-card pile, saying, "And four is nine."

Take the top card of this pile and place it to the right of the other two aces (Illus. 50).

Place the remaining cards in this pile on top of the deck, which you are still holding. Set the five-card pile on top of the deck.

Pick up the deck. "What's the lucky number?"

You must hope that she's knowledgeable enough to guess seven. If not, you'll have to tell her.

"Yes, seven is the number, Donna. So you'll need seven cards."

Fan out seven cards from the top of the deck and hand them to Donna.

"And who are the luckiest people in the world? The Australians. So I'd like you to give the cards the down-under shuffle. So put the top card down on the table, and then put the next one under—on the bottom of the deck."

She does this.

"The next one goes on top of the first card, and the next

one goes on the bottom. Continue on."

When she's done, the cards are in a pile on the table. Take the top card and place it to the right of the other three cards on the table (Illus. 51).

"Remember, Donna, you chose the numbers. Let's see how you did."

Turn the aces over one by one.

Note

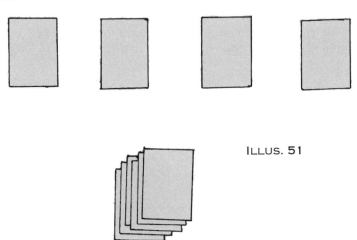

ILLUS. 51

After you have laid out the five-card piles and the smaller pile, don't say something like, "So we'll take your choice, the eighteenth card, and…"Why don't you say that? Because you're not taking the eighteenth card.

Regardless of the numbers chosen by Donna, in the first instance, you're taking the sixteenth card. In the second instance, you're taking the eleventh card. And in the third instance, you're taking the sixth card. It's best that the spectators not be made aware of this.

Kings in a Blanket

First, you must learn how to "fold the blanket." Start by dealing 16 cards face down, so that they form four rows and four columns (Illus. 52).

You can fold over any row or column and continue folding until you have just one pile of cards. How do you "fold over"? Simply turn over all the cards on one outside row or column and place them, reversed, on top of the cards next to them. Let's suppose that you turn over all the cards in the far right column and place each card on top of the card to its immediate left. The column on the right will now consist of four piles of two cards each; the bottom card of each pile will be face down and the top card face up.

You may continue by folding over the column on the right again, which would give you two columns, the one on the right consisting of four piles of three cards each.

ILLUS. 52

More than likely, however, you will decide to fold over a different outside row or column. After the first fold, suppose you decide to fold over the top row. The cards in the top row are turned over and placed face up onto the card directly beneath them. Now you would have three rows and three columns. The top row would now consist of three piles. The pile on the left and the one next to it would contain two cards each. The pile on the right would consist of four cards—the top card and the third card from the top being face up.

You would continue folding like this until only one pile remains. On with the trick.

Fan through the deck with the faces toward yourself. Place a few random cards on top. Explain, "I have to find certain cards or this will never work."

Continue fanning through. Place the four kings on top, one by one.

"All set," you declare. Turn the deck face down. The kings are now on the bottom of the 16-card pile.

Deal out the kings face down from the top of the deck so that they are roughly in the positions indicated by K's below. Deal out 12 more cards face down so that they fill the positions indicated by the O's below. Make sure that the kings are in the proper position.

O	O	K	K
O	O	O	O
K	O	O	K
O	O	O	O

"Hazel, I'd like you to watch carefully as I make a magic symbol on the blanket."

Turn over the cards indicated by X's in Illus. 53.

"Hazel, do you see the letter that the face-down cards make?" If she puzzles over it too long, add, "It makes the letter K, Hazel." Run over the face-down cards with your finger so that she can really see the K. "That K stands for King, Hazel. I'd

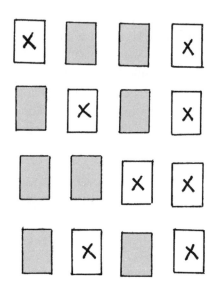

THE "K" IS FACING AWAY FROM YOU.

like you to remember that as you fold the blanket. Oh, that's right, I have to explain to you how to fold the blanket."

Explain how to Hazel. Believe me, it's much easier when you have the cards laid out. Explain to her the various options. Make sure she understands that she can fold it in any order she wishes. She can start at the bottom, then repeat with another bottom fold, or go anywhere else—whatever she wishes.

As she folds, you might well have to help her, making sure she doesn't goof up. When she's done, straighten out the single pile.

"Do you remember the magic sign I made on the blanket, Hazel?"

She does.

"And what did that letter K stand for?"

"King" she says.

"That's right." Pick up the pile. "Watch." Spread the pile out so that the four face-up kings show. As you spread the pile, you may see that a number of cards are face up. This means that you must turn the pile over to show the face-up kings.

BETTER THAN FOUR OF A KIND

Ken Beale had the original idea, and a mighty fine notion it is. I tossed in the ending, which I believe adds a stronger climax.

You must make a minor setup in advance. Remove from the deck the four aces and five spades: 6, 7, 8, 9, 10. Place the five spades face down on top of the deck in any order. On top of them, place the four aces face down.

Start by saying, "I'll teach you all to play Australian poker. We'll need the jacks for this."

Fan through the cards with the faces toward yourself, and toss out the jacks, face up, one by one. Put them into a row.

"The jacks, of course, are the critical cards. But we also need 12 additional cards."

Fan off three cards, even them up, and place them face down into a pile on the table, saying, "Three cards." Fan off two more cards, even them up, and place them on top of those on the table, saying, "And two is five." Deal one card on top of the others, saying, "And one is six."

Add, "And we'll need six more." Address Shirley, who has been very attentive: "We need six more, Shirley. How should we do it? Should I deal the way I did—three, two, one? Or should I deal one, two, three? Or should I just deal out six cards one at a time? It's up to you."

Deal the remaining six cards on top of the other six, in the manner directed. Set aside the rest of the deck.

Turn the jacks face down in place.

"To start with Australian poker, you must first deal the cards out in the regular way."

From left to right, deal a card on top of each of the jacks. Repeat three times, exhausting the cards you're holding. Pick up the pile on the far right. Place it onto the pile to the left of it. Place the combined pile onto the pile to its left. Place the combined pile onto the last pile on the left.

"Now we deal the cards in the Australian way, which is like this." Deal a card face down onto the table and put the next one under the packet. "Do you catch on, Shirley?" Pause. "One down and one under." She will probably tell you that the deal is, like Australia, "down under." If not, you tell her.

Continue by dealing a card face down onto the one on the table, and the next one under the packet. Continue until you hold only four cards. Turn them face up.

"There you are—the four jacks."

Set them aside, face up and spread out.

"So what do you do when an Australian is lucky enough to deal himself four jacks? I'll show you what I do. We'll do the down-under deal again."

Deal a card down, and put the next one under the packet. Continue until you hold only four cards. Turn them face up.

"There you are—the four aces. Now that's a real winner."

Place the aces aside near the jacks. Make sure they're face up and spread out.

"But if you really want to win, you should milk the cards—the American way."

Proceed to milk the cards as described in "Milking the Cards," on page 18. First, draw off the top and bottom cards together, placing the two face down onto the table. Again, draw off the top and bottom cards together, placing them on top of the two on the table.

"But in America, we need five cards."

Place the top card on top of the four cards on the table.

Set the remaining three cards on top of the deck that you set aside earlier. Pick up the five cards on the table. Hold them so that the faces are toward you. One by one, place the cards face up onto the table in this order: 6, 7, 8, 9, 10.

"There you are—a straight flush. I think that'll beat any four of a kind."

Notes

1) How is it that you can allow Shirley to direct the placement of the second six-card group? Simple. I figured out that whichever way you do it, the straight flush will be properly set up.

2) It takes quite a while to do the down-under shuffle, no matter how fast you go. So while you're dealing, converse about something. The best bet is to provide some amusing comments. You might discuss, among other things, the koala, the kangaroo, and anything else that begins with K. Or you might point out that you happen to know that the Outback is where they keep the barbie—whatever.

LUCKY CARD LOCATION

The spectator seems to make all the choices, yet you end up finding the chosen card. F. J. Baker had the original trick, which required a blank card. Since I seldom have one, I changed the handling slightly.

You must have a complete 52-card deck. Have Leonard shuffle the deck. Take the cards back, saying, "I have to find my lucky card. If all goes well, it will help with our next experiment." Fan through the cards with faces towards you. You must count to the twenty-fifth card. It will help allay spectator suspicion if you count the cards in groups of three. (Separate the cards after you count off 25.) The twenty-sixth card from the bottom is on the face of the pile in your left hand (Illus. 54).

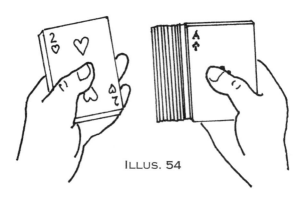

ILLUS. 54

"Here's my lucky card," you declare. Name the card. "If it's to do any good, we'll have to turn it over." Turn it over in place. Close up the cards. Turn the deck face down. The twenty-sixth card from the bottom is now face up in the face-down deck.

Hand the deck back to Leonard, saying, "Please think of a number from one to ten." Turn away. "Count off that number of cards from the top, and place them in your pocket or hide them somewhere else. I don't want to know your number." Pause. "Now look at the card that lies at that same number from the top and show it around. But make sure to keep it at that same number. For instance, if your number was three, you would look at the third card from the top. Be sure to remember that card because now that's your lucky card."

Turn back to the group. "We have my lucky card turned face up somewhere in the deck. Now let's try my lucky number. I wanted a lucky number that no one else had, so I chose 13. Please deal off 13 cards into a pile." Leonard does so. "Now into another pile, deal as many cards as you want, but make sure you deal past my lucky card, or this trick won't work."

When Leonard finishes, pick up the second pile he dealt and turn it face up. "Take the other pile, Leonard. Let's deal our cards into separate piles. I'll deal mine face up; you deal yours face down. We'll do it together so we match each other card for card. When we come to my face-down card, we'll stop." Immediately after dealing off your face-down card, stop the deal. Turn the card over, saying, "There it is...my lucky card." Ask him to name the card he chose. Point to the last card he dealt and ask him to turn it over. "Look at that—there's *your* lucky card."

PRINTS OF MAGIC

Walter Gibson invented the main idea; I've combined it with a wonderful old trick.

You must know the name of the top card. A good way is to sneak a peek at the bottom card and, in an overhand shuffle, bring that bottom card to the top of the deck. Ask Henry to think of any number from one to 20, and to deal off that many cards into a pile on the table.

"Now," you tell Henry, "cut the remainder of the deck into two piles." After he does so, ask him to shuffle one of the two piles. Then he is to shuffle the other pile. Finally, point to the pile he first dealt off. "Please pick up those cards and hold them facing you so that you can see the bottom card but I can't. Remember that bottom card. Now, if you don't mind, just put your thumb print on the face of that card, right around the middle."

Pick up one of the other two piles and show Henry exactly how to affix his thumb print (Illus. 55). Say, "I'll turn away while you put your thumb print on the face of your card." Turn away for a moment and give these instructions: "Now shuffle that pile. Then put it together with the other piles and give the entire deck a shuffle." The card he "chose" is, of course, the card you originally peeked at.

Turn back and take the pack from Henry. Turn the top card face up and ask Henry to put his right thumb print on the face of that card. (If it happens that the top card is the one he chose, take a bow and *quit!*) Stare at the card, ostensibly studying the thumb print. "Very interesting. Should be easy to identify."

Set the card face up on the table. Turn the deck face up and begin spreading the cards out, glancing back and forth from the deck to the thumb-printed card as you try to find a match. Act this out, pausing here and there to study a possibility. It works well to go *past* the chosen card and, after spreading out several more, go back to it. Pick it up and compare it closely with the other card. "An exact match!" you declare. "This must be your card."

COUNT OFF

I came across this trick in a magic magazine, where it was referred to as an "old trick." I performed it for several months, and then I realized that I had invented the trick decades earlier.

Over the years, however, someone had added a refinement which enhances the effect. Here's the new, improved version.

Have Lillian thoroughly shuffle the deck. Spread the cards out face up, showing how thoroughly the cards are mixed. Note the top and bottom cards. Add them together. Suppose the top card is a 5 and the bottom is a 7. The sum is 12. Turn the deck face down and start to spread the cards out, offering the choice of a card. As you do so, secretly count off 12 cards and hold these slightly separate from the rest (Illus. 56). (The number you count off is the same as the total of the top and bottom cards. When you count off the cards, count in groups of three.) Make sure the card is chosen from below these. After Lillian looks at the card and shows it around, lift off the top 12 cards and extend the rest of the deck for her to replace the card. Place the 12 cards on top, even up the deck, and set the deck on the table. From this point on, don't touch the cards.

It's time for a bit of distraction. Address the spectators: "The deck was thoroughly shuffled by Lillian, who then freely selected a card. I haven't changed the position of a single card in the deck. Yet if we're lucky, we'll see a miracle." Gesture towards the deck. "Lillian, please cut off a *large* chunk of cards."

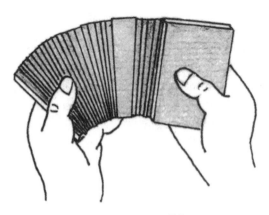

ILLUS. 56

You want to make sure she cuts off well over half the deck. "Notice...complete freedom of choice." Point to the small packet, the former lower portion of the deck. "Please turn this pile face up." Call attention to the value of the bottom card of the pile. "Now pick up the other packet and deal into a pile that same number of cards."

Now have her turn the dealt pile face up. She notes the value of the bottom card and deals that many into a third pile. This pile is also turned up, the bottom card noted, and that many dealt into yet another pile.

"Enough piles, right? So what was the name of the chosen card?" After it's named, have Lillian turn the last pile face up. There's the chosen card.

I am always a little surprised at the conclusion. *Three* different cards are counted off from a *shuffled* deck, and the chosen card is found.

Note

At the beginning, when you fan through to add the top and bottom cards, the total may be unusually high—20, for instance. When this occurs, have the cards reshuffled.

THE FOOLER

I call this trick *The Fooler* because magician Wally Wilson completely fooled me with this one. The secret is extremely subtle.

Ask Kevin to shuffle the deck thoroughly. "Now please think of a number from five to 15, and deal that many cards into a face-up pile." Start to turn away, but *before* your back is turned, catch a glimpse of the first card Kevin deals. That first card is your key card. That's it! You're all done with the sneaky portion of the trick.

"Look at the last card you dealt. That's your chosen card. In other words, your card is the one that's at your chosen number.

Now cut off a pile from the top of the deck and set it on the table. Pick up the cards you dealt off, turn them face down, and place them on top of the pile in your hands. Put the pile you cut off on top of all."

Turn back to the audience. "There's no doubt now that your chosen card is buried in the middle of the deck where I can't possibly find it." Have Kevin give the deck a few complete cuts.

Take the deck and fan the cards face up before you, staring at one and then another. No luck. Shake your head. "I can't seem to get a picture of your card. Maybe this will help.... What was the number you thought of?" Suppose Kevin tells you 13. Still puzzled, you fan back and forth through the face-up cards. When you spot your key card, start with that card and count 13 cards towards the face of the deck. The thirteenth one is the selected card.

Tentatively remove the card and place it face down on the table. "Maybe this is it. What was your card?" Success!

THE DIVINING ONE

To perform this, you'll need the assistance of five spectators. Ask one spectator to shuffle the deck and then deal it into five equal piles. He will, of course, have two cards left over. These are set aside.

Pick up one of the two cards, saying, "This will have to be my divining card. If all goes well, it will help me find the selected cards." Sneak a look at the face of the card as you touch it to the top of each of the piles (Illus. 57). This is your key card. Then, as you continue speaking, casually set the card a few inches on the far side of the other card. "I'd like five different people to each look at the top card of one of these piles. Remember that card and place it back on top of its pile."

After they've done so, have a spectator gather up the piles one on top of the other. As he starts, pick up the closest card

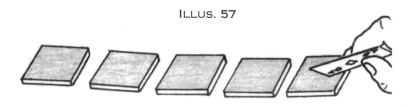

to you of the two on the table. (The other is the one you secretly peeked at.) "I'll need the divining card," you say, "but you might as well set the other card in there." Chances are that he'll place that other card on the top or bottom of one of the piles as he gathers the cards up. If he seems about to push it *into* a pile, however, you must instantly say, "Just put it on top of any of the piles."

Once the cards are gathered, each of the participants gives the deck a complete cut. Spread the deck face up on the table. Pass the "divining card" over the spread several times. "I think I'm getting the right vibrations," you say. Set the card down. Close up the deck, pick it up, and fan it, faces towards you. Find your key card. Cut the deck so that it becomes the bottom card—that is, the card on the face of the deck. Remove the top card of the deck, touch it to the "divining card," and say, "Yes, that's one." Place the card face down on the table.

Every tenth card after your key card is one of those selected. So, with the cards facing you, fan through from the bottom, casually counting to the tenth card *after* the key card. When you remove this one card, separate the pile you've fanned off so that you'll know where to start the next count. As you locate each card, touch it to the divining card, mumble your approval, and place the card face down on the table.

Finally, turn one of the cards on the table face up. Suppose it is the queen of hearts. "Who had the queen of hearts?" Hand it to the spectator who replies. Repeat with the other four cards.

POKER LOCATION

Milt Kort called my attention to this old trick. This version is by Hen Fetsch; I made some minor simplifications.

The trick is performed while you and the spectators are seated at a table.

Ask a spectator to shuffle the deck and place it on the table. Say to the spectator, "Please cut off half the deck and place it on the table." Point to the former lower section of the deck, and ask the spectator on your left to take the top card of this section. Working clockwise, you have three more spectators each remove a card from the top of this pile. Finally, *you* take one from the top of the pile. "Everyone please look at your card and remember it." You do likewise.

Place your card back on top of the pile. Going *counterclockwise*, the spectators replace their cards on top. Have someone put either pile on top of the other. Each participant gives the pack a complete cut.

Take the pack. Fan through it, faces towards yourself, saying, "I need to find my lucky poker card. In a game of five-card stud, I once filled a straight flush with this...Ah, there it is—my lucky poker card!" Name the card.

Actually, you fan through to the card you took from the deck. Count this card as "one," and continue counting as you push the cards into your right hand one by one. When you reach card number 15, stop. Cut the cards so that card number 15 becomes the top card of the deck. Call attention to the bottom (face) card of the deck, calling it, as above, your lucky poker card. Toss the card face up onto the middle of the table.

The chosen cards should now be 11th, 12th, 13th, 14th, and 15th from the top. Deal out five poker hands in the regular way, the last hand going to yourself. Ask the spectators not to look at their cards. Make sure the cards are kept in a pile in the order in which they're dealt.

Each spectator picks up his hand, holding it face down.

Then demonstrate with your cards as you give these instructions: "Don't peek at your cards. Now please move your top card to the bottom. Turn the next card face up and put it on top of my lucky poker card on the table. The next card goes to the bottom, and the next one goes face up on top of my lucky poker card. Keep going until you have only one card left."

When all are finished, declare the name of your chosen card and turn it over. Ask the spectator on your left what his card was. Have him turn it over. Do the same for the other three spectators. Each is left with his selected card.

Note

As explained, the trick is performed with four spectators. You may, however, perform it with either more or fewer. In the version above, you find your lucky poker card (the card you originally took from the deck). Counting this card as "one," you count off a total of 15, and cut the cards so that card number 15 becomes the top card of the deck. The number 15 is derived by multiplying the total number of hands by three.

As described above, five hands are dealt, so the number used is 15. Suppose only three spectators are assisting. Only four hands would be dealt. Multiply that by three, and you get 12. So instead of 15, you use the number 12.

If five spectators are helping, you'll have a total of six hands. Six times three is 18, which is the number you'll use.

It's Nice to See Your Back

This trick was originated by Ben Christopher and expanded by Roy Walton.

A little preparation is necessary. Suppose you're working with a blue-backed deck. Take a card from a red-backed deck. Remove the duplicate of that card from the blue-backed deck. Now place the red-backed card fifteenth from the bottom of your deck. You're ready to perform.

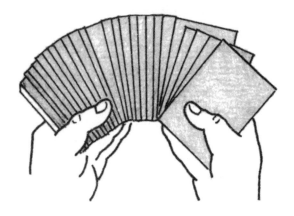

Remove the deck from its case and fan out about half the cards face down, saying, "We're going to have two of you merely *think* of cards from this deck" (Illus. 58). Close up the deck. You've subtly put across the point that the backs are all the same.

Ask Molly to cut off a small packet of cards from the top. Turn the deck face up and have Dora cut off a small packet from the bottom. (Make sure both spectators cut off fewer than 15 cards.) Ask Molly and Dora to turn away and secretly count their cards.

"Both of you have counted your cards, so each of you now has a number in mind." Turn to Molly. Ask her to note and remember the card that lies at her number. From the face-up deck, count aloud as you deal 14 cards into a pile on the table, reversing their order. Molly now has her card. Pick up the pile and replace it on the face of the pack.

Ask Dora to note and remember the card that lies at her number. Deal and count aloud 14 cards, exactly as before. Pick up the 14-card packet and place it *beneath* the face-up deck.

Still holding the cards face up, say, "We'd better have a complete deck." Hold out your hand to Molly. She gives you her packet of cards, which you place *beneath* the face-up deck. Dora's packet goes on top of the face-up deck.

Spread the pack face up on the table. "Sometimes one card will stand out from the others," you explain. "I hope that's the case." Separate various cards, moving your hand back and forth over the spread. Actually, you're counting down to the fifteenth card from the top. Eventually, push this one card out of line, saying, "This one really stands out." Address Molly. "Does this happen to be your card?" It does.

Close up the spread and pick up the cards. Turn the pack face down. "Sometimes you can get an even stronger impression by studying the backs of the cards." Spread out the pack face down. One red-backed card stands out among the blue backs. Push this card out of line. Ask Dora, "What was the name of your card?" She names it and you turn it over.

THE TEN-CARD TRICK

A favorite of Harry Blackstone, Sr., this trick can involve as many as five spectators. Three, however, seems to work best for me. I've added a few touches.

Assume you're going to get three spectators to assist you, Jim, Tom, and Sam. Ask one of them to shuffle the deck and take any ten cards for himself. Have the other spectators do the same. Take the remaining cards and set them aside.

"When I turn away, I'd like each of you to think of a number from one to ten. Then fan through your cards and see which card lies at that number from the top. Please remember your card *and* your number."

When you turn back, you will, in effect, transfer five cards from the top to the bottom of each spectator's pile. What you actually do is transfer 15 cards from the top to the bottom in a phony shuffle.

Take Jim's packet, saying, "I'd better mix these a bit." Transfer cards from the top to the bottom of the packet, moving one, two, or three cards each time. As you do so, silently keep track. When you have transferred fifteen, quit. Return the packet to Jim. Quickly perform the same "shuffle" for Tom and Sam and return their packets.

Since the number you move each time is arbitrary, it appears that you're actually mixing the cards. In no time, you will be so used to the procedure that you can actually chat while doing it.

"Do you all remember your number? Good. I'll turn away once more. Then I'd like each of you to transfer that number of cards from the top to the bottom of your pile. For instance, if your number was four, you would move four cards from the top to the bottom *one at a time!*"

This time when you turn back, say, "I'd like each of you to take your top card and place it on the bottom. Then deal the next one onto the table. Then the next one goes on the bottom; the next on the table. Continue until you have just one card left. But please don't peek at that last card. Just hang on to it."

Finally, each spectator is holding one card face down. Ask Jim to name his selected card and then to turn over the one he's holding. Have Tom and Sam do the same. Naturally, each is holding his chosen card.

COMPUTER WHIZ

Robert Neale invented this basic trick, using only the kings and queens. I added eight more cards, along with a few new notions, and ended up with a routine featuring three big surprises. It's an interesting, unusual, and colorful trick. Dan Harlan suggested that I add a new ending to the trick, and mentalist Marv Long offered a patter suggestion that brought everything together.

"I'd like to tell you about my new computer dating service," you announce as you begin fanning through the deck, faces towards yourself. Remove the face cards and the tens from the deck, tossing them face up onto the table. "I'm taking all the ladies and gentlemen from the deck. The kings and jacks are men, of course. And the queens are women. But, of course, the tens are also women.

By this time you should have the kings, queens, jacks, and tens lying face up on the table. Set the rest of the deck aside. Gather up the group on the table and fan them out, faces towards yourself. Now place two face-down piles onto the table. (At the end, I'll explain how I do this and how the setup can be easily memorized.) In one pile, these should be the face-down cards, *from the bottom up* (the king of spades being the bottom card):

KS QS JC 10C 10D JD QH KH

In the other pile, these are the face-down cards, *from the bottom up*:

KC QC JS 10S 10H JH QD KD

As you perform the setup, explain, "We're going to computerize the names of these ladies and gentlemen, so that they can be retrieved whenever we wish. In other words, we're installing them on the hard drive." When the two piles are arranged on the table, ask Edith to help out.

Turn away and say to her, "Now we want to have our first customer of the computer dating service. So please pick up one of the piles, Edith, and fan it out so that you can see all the cards. Then just *think* of one of the cards. It can be either a man or a woman; it can be a red or a black card. In other words, it can be a person with either red hair or black hair. When you have your card, close up the fan and put that pile on top of the other one."

Turn back and pick up the packet on the table. "Now we must program the computer. As you know, computers work on

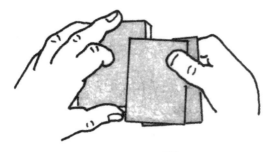

ILLUS. 59

a binary system, so all our programming will be based on the number two. For instance, you had a choice of *two* piles."

Hold the packet from above in your left hand. With the thumb and fingers of your right hand, draw off the top and bottom cards together (Illus. 59). This is known as *milking* the deck (see page 18). Place the two cards face down to the left. Again draw off the top and bottom cards together. Place them to the right of the first pile of two cards. "Milk" the next two cards from the packet and place them on top of the pile on the left. The next two are "milked" and placed onto the pile on the right. Continue alternating like this until all the cards are placed into two piles.

Pick up one of the piles and fan out the cards with the faces towards Edith. "Is your card here?" you ask. Whatever she answers, the pile containing her card must go *on top of* the other pile. If she says no, close up the cards, pick up the pile on the table and place it on top of the one in your hand. If she says yes, close up the cards and drop them on top of the pile on the table. Pick up the packet.

"We need to feed the computer more information." Holding the packet in the dealing position in your left hand, push off the top two cards and raise them above the others about half of their length. Push off the next two cards, and lower them so that they extend below the first two about half their length. Push off the next two and raise them as you did the first pair (Illus. 60). The next two are pushed off and lowered as you did with the second pair. Continue through the packet, alternating up and down pairs.

ILLUS. 60

When you finish, with your palm-down right hand grasp the raised group and pull (or strip) them from the others (Illus. 61). Still holding the lower group in your left hand, fan out the other eight cards so that Edith can see the faces (Illus. 62). (If this move is uncomfortable, set the cards which are in your left hand onto the table while you do the fanning.) Ask Edith if her card is in the group you're showing her. Whatever she answers, remember that the group in which her card lies must go *beneath* the other group.

Repeat the up-and-down procedure with the cards and, again, strip out the upper group. Show this group to Edith and ask if her card is there. This time, the group in which her card lies goes *on top* of the other group.

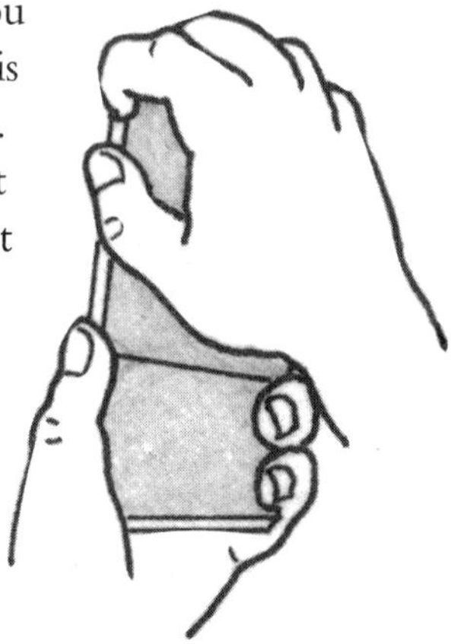

ILLUS. 61

At the very beginning of the trick, the group from which Edith selects a card goes on top. After you milk the cards, the group in which her card lies goes on top. With the first up-and-down maneuver, the group in which her card lies goes *beneath* the other group. In the second up-and-down maneuver, the group in which her card lies goes on top. In other words, the only time her pile goes beneath the other pile is when you do the *first* up-and-down maneuver.

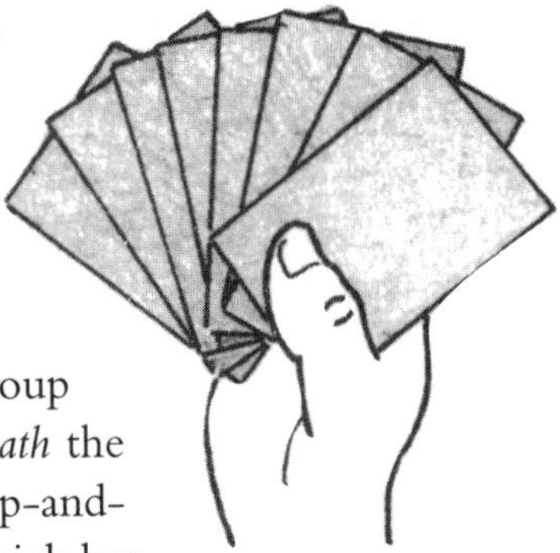

ILLUS. 62

"We're almost done programming," you say, "and we're still using the binary system." Fan off the top two cards of the deck and place them onto the table, keeping them in the same order. Fan off the next two and place them to the right of the first two. Fan off the next two and place them on top of the first pair. Fan off the next two and place them on top of the second pair. Continue alternating like this until all 16 cards have been placed into two piles.

"The computer is ready. I think it'd be wonderful if the computer could provide us with the name of the card you chose to be our first customer. But my program is set up so that it'll only provide information bit by bit—or byte by byte. I'm going to ask you some questions. You can lie or tell the truth—it doesn't matter. The computer has been fed the proper information, and it never misses. Well, hardly ever. First question: What sex is the card you thought of? Was it a man, like a king or jack? Or was it a woman, like a queen or 10?"

Edith answers. Lift off the *top card* of the pile on the right, turn it over, and display it, still holding it. Toss it forward face up, as though dealing it. (This is the only time you use the top card of the pile on the right; the rest of the time, you turn the entire pile over.) It will give the proper sex of the chosen card. (If the card was a king, for example, this card would be a jack.) Comment on Edith's veracity. If she lied, for instance, tell her that she can't possibly fool the computer.

Casually turn over the card you tossed out face up, pick up the remainder of the pile on the right, and place it onto the card. This pile should be placed forward and to the left.

Pick up the remaining eight-card pile and deal it into two piles, two cards at a time, just as you did before. "Next question: What color is your card—red or black? In other words, was it a person with black hair or red hair?" After she answers, turn over the pile on the right, showing the bottom card. This will be the proper color. (If she chose a heart, for example, this would be a diamond.) Make a comment on the unerring accuracy of the computer as you turn the pile face down and set it *to the right* of the first pile you discarded.

Pick up the remaining four-card pile and deal it into two piles as before. "What was the suit of your card?" you ask. After she responds, you provide the correct answer by turning over the pile on the right. Turn this pair face down and place it to the right of the other two discarded piles.

You have two cards remaining. Deal the first to the left and the second to the right. "What was the value of your card?" The card on the right discloses the correct value. Turn this card face down and set it a bit to one side.

"So what was the name of your card?" The remaining card is it. Turn it over and leave it in place.

"So we've found the person you chose, but we haven't found her (him) a date." Suppose the chosen card is the queen of hearts. "So we have this lovely lady. We should line her up with at least four possible dates. Do you think she would prefer men with black hair or men with red hair?"

Here's the situation: On the table you have three piles of cards. The pile on the left, Pile 1, has eight cards. The pile to the right of it, Pile 2, has four cards. And the pile on the far right, Pile 3, has two cards. In addition, you have a face-down card you have set a bit to one side, and you have the face-up chosen card.

Edith chooses. Suppose she elects to have men with red hair. Red is the same color as the selected card. When someone selects the same color as the selected card, you proceed as follows:

Pick up the chosen card, turn it face down, and place it on top of Pile 1. Pick up Pile 1 and place it onto Pile 2. Place the combined piles onto Pile 3. Place all on top of the card you set aside. (The piles will always be gathered up, with Pile 1 going onto Pile 2, and the combined pile going onto Pile 3.)

"Let's see if the computer can generate some dates for the young lady." As before, fan off the top two cards of the deck and place them onto the table, keeping them in the same order. In the same way, deal off two cards to the right of these. Two more are dealt onto the pile on the left, and then two more onto the pile on the right. You've now dealt eight cards, four in each pile. Just as you dealt these cards, deal the remaining eight cards into two piles that are forward of the first two.

Turn over the top card of each packet. In the example, you'll have two red jacks and two red kings.

When someone selects the color opposite that of the selected card, proceed as follows:

Place the card you set aside on top of Pile 2. Turn the chosen card face down and place it on top of Pile 2. (Pile 2 now has the chosen card on top; below it is the card you set aside; below these two are four more cards.) Gather up the piles and deal them out, as explained—that is, Pile 1 goes onto Pile 2, and the combined pile goes onto Pile 3. Then four piles are formed, as described above. The four top cards are turned over. In this event, the four cards would be two black jacks and two black kings.

You might comment, "Who could ask for more—four handsome men (beautiful ladies) to choose from?"

Now for the finale. Edith has chosen the queen of hearts. Four piles are on the table. Edith had her choice of either red-haired men or black-haired men, so face up on top of the piles are either the black jacks and kings, or the red jacks and kings. Let's say that Edith picked red-haired men.

"Edith, let's suppose you have your choice of these handsome men. Would you pick one of them up, please?" She does so. Four piles are on the table; on top of three of these is a face-up card. Turn the face-up cards face down. Here's the placement of the piles as you look at them:

3   4

1   2

Earlier, Edith chose either red-haired or black-haired persons. If Edith selected persons of the same color as the chosen card, that card is now second from the bottom in Pile 1. If Edith selected persons with a different hair color, the chosen card is second from the bottom in Pile 3.

"Let's try an experiment. We'll let you do the programming."

Pick up the pile containing the chosen card, and hold that pile face down in the left hand. Say to Edith, "Which pile should go on next?" Whichever she chooses, place it on top of the cards in your left hand. Have her choose another pile and place that one on top. Then place the remaining pile on top.

Say, "You'll have to do some more programming. We'll have to put your potential date into the program. I'm going to form two piles. I'd like you to drop the card you're holding on top of one of the piles whenever you wish. Make sure you drop it face up."

Now you're going to "milk" the cards, as explained earlier.

Hold the packet from above in the left hand, and draw off the top and bottom cards together with your right hand. Drop these two onto the table. Draw off the top and bottom cards again, and place these to the right of the other pile. In the same way, add two to the pile on the left, and then add two to the pile on the right. Continue until Edith drops her cards on top of one of the piles. At this point, the original chosen card is on the bottom of the pile on the right.

Suppose, however, that Edith doesn't drop her card onto one of the piles. You'll end up placing a single card on top of the pile on the right. Place the pile on the left on top of the pile on the right. Explain, "Now you're to drop your card face up on top of one of the piles as I deal them." Again milk the cards; this time, the original chosen card will be on the bottom of the pile on the left.

At last Edith places the face-up card on top of one of the piles. Stop dealing immediately.

There are now two possibilities:

1) If Edith places the card on top of the pile which has the chosen card on the bottom, have her give that pile a complete cut. Place the cards in your hand onto the table. Say, "Please reassemble the cards. Just place any packet on top of another, and then place those on top of the remaining packet. Do it any way you wish."

2) If Edith places the card on top of the pile that *doesn't* have the chosen card on the bottom, have her place *either pile* on top of the other. She then gives the pile a complete cut. If the cut brings the face-up card to the top or bottom, have her cut again. Place the cards in your hand on the table. Say, "Please put one of the piles on top of the other."

The cards are now assembled, and the face-up card is face to face with the original chosen card.

"You're the programmer this time," you say. "You've been making the choices. Complete the programming by giving the cards one more complete cut." Again, if the face-up card comes to the top or bottom, have Edith cut again.

Let's return to our example. Fan through the cards to the face-up card. Remove it, along with the card above it, and place the pair onto the table. The chosen card is face down on top of the face-up card. "Edith, you originally chose the queen of hearts. And you had four men to choose from. You chose this man." Name the card. "Let's see if this computer dating system really works. Did he also choose you?" Turn the chosen card face up. "Yes! The queen of hearts! I can't believe it. The system actually works. And *you* are a superb programmer."

Note

Here's an easy way to set up the cards. Hold all 16 cards fanned out in your left hand, faces towards you. The first eight you'll choose are:

$$KS \ QS \ JC \ 10C \ 10D \ JD \ QH \ KH$$

Note that the first four go from king down to 10, and the next four go from 10 up to king. All you really need to remember is that the first black card is the king of spades and the first red card is the 10 of diamonds. The suits run in pairs, and all four suits are represented. First come four blacks and then four reds.

So you take out the king of spades and place it face down onto the table. On top of it, place another spade, the queen. You need two more blacks: first the jack of clubs, then the 10 of clubs. The sequence now reverses, starting with a ten, the 10 of diamonds. This is followed by the jack of diamonds. Then come two more reds. Since you must have all four suits, these must be the queen of hearts and the king of hearts.

You're done with Pile 1.

These are the cards in Pile 2:

$$KC \ QC \ JS \ 10S \ 10H \ JH \ QD \ KD$$

This pile is easy. First come the black cards, running from king down to ten. Then come the red cards, running from 10 up to king. The king of clubs is the first card placed face down onto the table, and the king of diamonds is the card on top of the pile.

IT'S A DAN-DY

Dan Harlan gave me permission to include this "mathematical" trick. I've included two variations. The principle is similar to that used in the previous trick, but the concept is totally different.

You can perform the trick for several spectators at the same time, but for clarity I'll first explain how you might do it for one person.

Let's assume Frank is assisting you. After he shuffles the pack, have him count off 15 cards. He looks through the 15 cards and thinks of one, after which he shuffles the packet.

Take the packet from him and explain, "I'm going to show you some cards and ask if your card is among them. Whether the answer is yes or no, I'll *always* place that bunch *under* the others. Please remember, I'll always place the cards you look at under the others."

Hold the packet face down. You'll now perform a stripping action similar to that used in *Computer Whiz* (page 121). Alternately push the cards up and down; only instead of pushing two cards each time, you'll only push one. Fan through the cards, pushing the first one up for half its length, the second one down, the third one up, the fourth down, and so on, until you finish the packet.

Then, with your palm-down right hand grasp the upper group and pull (or strip) them from the others (Illus. 61, page 124). Still holding the other group in your left hand, fan out the eight cards so that Frank can see them (Illus. 62, page 125).

"Is your card among these?" you ask. Whatever he answers, you place this eight-card packet below the others. Again, go through the up-and-down procedure, strip out the eight upper cards, and show them to Frank. Whatever his reply, the eight again go below the others. Repeat this two more times—four times in all. Then announce the exact number of Frank's card from the top. Count down to that number in the packet and show that you're correct.

How do you do it? Simply remember this geometric progression: one, two, four, eight. When you show the cards the first time, if the spectator answers yes, you remember one, the first number in the progression. On the second showing, if he says yes, add 2 to his total. Each time he answers no, you add *nothing* (that should be easy to remember). On the third showing, add 4 if he says yes. On the fourth showing, add 8 if he says yes.

Let's try an example. Show the spectator the cards the first time. He doesn't see his card. Place these cards under the others and remember *zero*. The spectator sees his card in the second group; you remember the number two. The third time the spectator also sees his card; you add 4 to the previous 2 and get 6. Show cards for the fourth time and the spectator doesn't see his card; this means another *zero*. The total, then, is 6. Announce to the spectator, "I believe that your card is the sixth card down." Count down to the sixth card and show that you're right.

That's the trick in its simplest form. The trick can be made more interesting, more amusing, and *easier* by having two or three spectators participate. (And, in the notes at the end, there's an intriguing version for *one* spectator.) Basically, you make a game of it. Here's how it works.

Frank and Lena agree to help out. "We're going to play a little game to see who can get the most points," you say. But first you have the pack shuffled and 15 cards counted off. While your back is turned, each of the spectators removes one card from the packet and remembers it. The cards are returned, and each of the spectators shuffles the packet.

Turn back to the group, take the packet, and continue, "I'm

going to show you some of these cards. If you see your card in that group, you get a point. If you don't, you get nothing. We'll do this several times." In this version, you *don't* mention that each time you will place the packet under the rest of the cards.

Do the up-down maneuver. Show the eight cards to Frank, asking if his card is there. Show them to Lena, asking if she sees her card. Suppose Frank sees his card and Lena doesn't see hers. "Ah, Frank, you have one point. And Lena, you have none. So Frank is ahead one to nothing. Let's raise the ante. This time, you get two points if you see your card."

Again, do the up-down maneuver. Let's say that both spectators see their card. "So that's two points apiece. Frank, you now have three points, and Lena has two. Let's raise it again. This time, we'll make it four points."

After the up-down maneuver, Frank doesn't see his card, but Lena sees hers. "You still have three points, Frank. And now Lena has four more points. She had one; now she has five. Finally, we'll give each of you a chance to get eight points."

Frank sees his card, but Lena doesn't see hers. "Let's see, you had three points, Frank. You now have eight more. This gives you eleven points. I'm sorry, Lena, but you lose. You still have only five points." Pause. "Five points. Let's see what card number five is." Count aloud as you deal off five cards. Ask Lena to name her card. Turn over the last card dealt off; it's hers. Turn Lena's card face down. Return the entire pile of five cards to the top of the packet.

"And, Frank, you had 11 points. Let's see what card 11 is." Count down to that card in the same way, ask the name of his selected card, and show it.

Clearly, you always count to the lower number first.

You can repeat the trick, since it's unlikely that the numbers will recur. You can readily perform with as many as three or four spectators. It's easy to keep track because each spectator will keep a running total of his own score. If you should happen to forget, feel free to ask. It also helps if you keep repeating the score as you go along.

Notes

This trick definitely bears repetition. Do it *at least* twice.

When performing with one spectator, I find it works well to play the same game with *me* as the opponent. Start by proposing that you and the spectator have a contest to see who can get the most points. She shuffles the pack and counts off 15 cards. Take the 15 cards, saying, "First, I'll think of one of these cards." Actually, you fan through and *pretend* to think of one. Give the packet back, have her shuffle and think of one of the cards herself. Again she shuffles the packet.

Take the packet and turn it face up. Fan out several cards from the top of the face-up packet, saying, "Thoroughly mixed." With a quick glance down, note the second card from the top of the face-up packet. (This will be the second card from the bottom when you turn the packet face down.) Look away and casually fan out a few more cards. The card you noted will be the card you "thought of." Close up the packet and turn it face down.

Perform the up-down maneuver. As always, strip out the upper group and show this group to the spectator. "If you see your card, you get a point. If not, I get a point," you explain. Keep a running total of the comparative score as you show the cards four times. As before, the progression is one, two, four, eight.

Suppose that at the completion of the game, the spectator has nine points. (You'll have six in this instance, because the total will always be 15.) Congratulate the spectator on her victory. Then say, "You had nine points. Let's check the ninth card." Count eight cards into a pile, one on top of the other, and toss out the ninth card. Ask the name of her card and have her turn over the one you tossed out. As she turns it over, drop the cards in your hand on top of the pile on the table. Take her chosen card, turn it face down, and drop it on top of the stack.

"My number was six," you say. Count off six cards. Name the card you'd peeked at. Turn it over. Sure enough, yours came out also.

Once in a blue moon, the spectator will choose the same card as you do. At the end, when she names her card, simply say, "What a coincidence! That's the same card I thought of." Then repeat the trick.

MAGIC SPELLS

IT'S MAGIC

The originator of this trick is (I believe) Patrick Duffie. Milt Kort introduced the trick to me.

Set a thoroughly shuffled deck on the table. Ask Felix and Louise to help out. Say to Felix, "Please cut the deck into three fairly equal piles." When he's done, address Louise: "Choose one of those piles, and put the other two back into the card case."

About one third of the deck is left on the table. Ask Louise to cut off a small pile from the packet. Felix takes the remaining cards.

Say to Louise, who has the smaller packet, "If I should perform a mysterious feat, would you say, 'It's magic.'?" Whatever she replies, continue, "I'd like you to look at the bottom card of your packet, Louise. That's your chosen card." When she has done so, say, "Now spell out the words 'It's magic,' moving one card from the top to the bottom of your packet for each letter in the spelling."

Guide her through this.

Turn your attention to Felix. "You don't believe in magic, do you, Felix? You think all of this is trickery. In fact, you think that this is a dumb trick. What I'd like you to do is look at the bottom card of your packet and remember it." When he's done so, say, "Now please spell out the sentence 'This is a dumb trick.' Just as Louise did, move one card from the top to the bottom of your packet for each letter in the spelling."

Guide Felix as well.

"Time for some elimination. I'd like each of you to deal your top card onto the table. Now place your next card underneath the packet. The next card goes on the table, and the next on the bottom of the packet. Keep going until you have only one card left, but please don't look at the card."

Help out as they perform their "down-and-under" deal. At

last, each is holding one card face down.

"From the beginning, I haven't touched the cards, right? Nor did I have any way of knowing how many cards each of you would choose. So let's see if I'm magical…or not." Ask Louise to name her card. She then turns her last card over; it's the one she chose. Repeat the procedure with Felix.

Notes

The smaller pile must consist of no more than eight cards, and the larger no more than 16 cards. If you follow the above routine exactly, the numbers should work out.

You can work up a patter of your own, if you wish. Any eight-letter sentence will do for the smaller packet, and any 16-letter sentence will work for the larger packet.

In some respects the trick is even more effective when performed for one spectator. After you've eliminated two thirds of the pack, the spectator cuts off a small pile from the remaining third. Offer the choice of the smaller packet or the larger packet. The pile which isn't chosen is placed in the card case with the other cards. Clearly, you proceed with the spectator looking at the bottom card and then spelling out "It's magic" with the smaller pile, or "This is a dumb trick" with the larger pile. This is followed by the down-and-under deal and the revelation of the chosen card.

Lots of Luck

Magician Wally Wilson showed me a spelling trick that he'd invented. I worked out a way to accomplish a similar effect using a different principle.

Margie's a good sport, so ask her to shuffle the deck. Take it back, saying, "Poker is a game in which luck plays an important part, and we're going to need all kinds of luck for this experiment to work." Quickly push off five groups of five cards, tossing them on the table.

"Now we have five poker hands. Please pick up one of the hands, look it over, and take any card from it. Please show that card to everyone but me." Take the other four cards from her and place them on top of the deck. Continue: "Place the chosen card on top of one of the other piles, and place one of the remaining piles on top."

At this point, there are three piles on the table: two five-card piles and one 11-card pile in which the chosen card lies sixth from the top. You're holding the deck.

Spread the deck out face down directly in front of Margie. As you now speak, casually straighten the piles and place the two five-card piles on top of the 11-card pile. "I'd like you to draw out one card from the deck, but don't look at it just yet. Any card at all."

After Margie draws out the card, take the deck from her and set it on the table. Pick up the combined piles and drop them on top of the deck.

"Now we're going to spell out the name of the card you just picked out. We'll deal off one card for each letter in the spelling. We'll spell out the name of the card *exactly*. For example, if you picked the queen of diamonds, we'd spell out (slowly) *queen of diamonds*. Don't worry, I'll show you how to do it."

Have her turn over the card. "Here's how you do it." Deal a card into a pile for each letter in the spelling of the card. Leaving the pile on the table, hand her the remainder of the deck. "Now you do it."

After she spells out the name of the card, take the deck from her and place it on top of the pile you spelled out. "We'll have to get rid of some more cards," you explain. "Pick up your pile, please. Now place the top card on the bottom. Then place the next card on the table." After she does so, say, "The next one on the bottom, and the next one on the table." She continues like this until only one card remains in her hand. Stop her, making sure she doesn't turn over the card.

"What's the name of your chosen card?" She gives the name; it's the card in her hand.

SIMPLE SPELLER

The first part of this trick can be done facing the spectators, but I prefer to turn my back. Ask Annette to help by shuffling the deck. Turn away and give the following instructions:

"Annette, look through the deck and find any two spot cards. Place them face up on the table, side by side. Now deal face-down cards on each one so that the total will equal ten. For instance, if you have a 7 face up, you would deal a card face down on it, saying eight...deal another, saying nine...and a final card, saying ten—a total of ten. Do this for both cards."

Pause.

"Notice the total of the two face-up cards. Deal that many into a separate pile from the top of the deck. Now look at the top card of the deck and show it around. That's your chosen card. Replace it on top of the deck and put the deck on the table. Pick up the pile you counted off, mix it up, and put the cards on top of the deck. You have two small piles left on the table. Turn down the face-up card in each pile. Mix the two piles together and place the cards on top of the deck."

Turn back to the group. Address Annette: "Why have I had you go through all this? Two reasons: So that you would have complete freedom of choice, and so that the position of the card in the deck would be a complete mystery to me. Therefore, we must resort to magic."

Since the trick is completely self-working, you could simply proceed. But it's best to give the spectators something extra to think about. I usually take the pack, give it one "magic riffle," and return it to my helper. All I do is riffle the ends of the deck upwards.

"I'd like you to spell out a sentence," I say, "dealing out one card for each letter. Here's the sentence: 'The next card will be yours.'"

Guide her through it. Naturally, when she finishes the spelling, you have her turn over the next card. That's it all right.

Note

Any 22-letter sentence will work. You can improvise a sentence using the spectator's name, for instance.

NUMBER, PLEASE

Bill Logan invented this clever trick, which can be repeated successfully a number of times. I've simplified the calculations to make it easier for you to do the trick, and to make it *possible* for me to do it.

The effect is this: A spectator lays out cards on the table to represent a freely chosen seven-digit telephone number. Quickly gather up the cards one by one, occasionally cutting the small face-up packet. Turn the cards face down and, one at a time, *spell out* the digits in the number, moving one card from the top to the bottom for each letter in the spelling. In each instance, the last card in the spelling is turned face up and dropped on the table. Each time it's the card representing the correct digit.

Start by asking a spectator to think of any seven-digit telephone number. Have him remove cards from the deck to represent that number, laying them in a face-up row on the table. A zero would be represented by any face card, and a one by an ace. Assume that he chose the seven-digit number 651-7082. On the table he'd lay out these cards of any suits:

6   5   A   7   (face card)   8   2

Before continuing, consider this: The *value* of any card can be spelled out in three, four, or five letters. Your job is to arrange these particular cards so that they can be spelled out in order.

To start, pick up the last card in the telephone number. Pick up the 2 and place it face up in your left hand. Then pick up the second-to-last card. Note how many letters are in the name of the card. If the number of letters is even (four, five, nine, or zero), place it on top of the card in your left hand. But if the number of letters is odd (one, two, three, six, seven, or eight), place it beneath the card in your left hand.

In our example, first the 2 is placed face up in the left hand. Then pick up the 8 and note that it's spelled in five letters (an odd number), so place it face up *beneath* the 2.

Continue picking up cards and adding them to those in your left hand, following these rules:

Pick up the cards in reverse order.

Place each card face up on top of the face-up cards in your left hand.

Each time you do so, note how many letters are in the name of the face-up card. Divide the number of cards now in your hand *into* this number.

1) If there's a remainder, move that number of cards from the face of the face-up pile to the bottom. (Cards may be moved singly or in a group. *Don't* count them off one on top of the other and then move them.)

2) If there's no remainder, leave the packet as it is.

3) Suppose the number of cards in the packet is *larger* than the number of letters in the name of the card. Simply move to the bottom of the face-up packet a number of cards equal to the number of letters in the name of the card.

Let's get back to our example. In your left hand is a face-up 2 and, below it, a face-up 8. Now continue to pick up cards in reverse order. Pick up the face card, which represents zero, and place it on those in your left hand. You now hold three cards in your left hand, and the top card, zero, is spelled in four letters. Divide 3 into 4, and you have a remainder of 1. Move one card (the face card) beneath the others.

Pick up the 7 and place it on top of the face-up packet in your left hand. This make four cards in the packet. The word seven is spelled in five letters. Divide 4 into 5, and again you have a remainder of 1. Once more, move one card from the face of the packet to the bottom.

Pick up the ace (which is considered a one) and place it on top of the pile in your left hand, bringing the total number of cards to five. *One* has three letters. Five is greater than this, so move three cards to the bottom of the packet.

In the next two instances, the number of cards in the pile will always be greater than the number of letters in the card placed on the face of the pile. In our example, place the 5 on the packet. Since "five" is spelled in four letters, move four cards to the bottom of the packet.

After placing the 6 on the packet, move three cards to the bottom (the same number as that used in spelling 6).

Turn the packet face down. You're ready to spell out the telephone number in order. In the example, the number is 651-7082, so you first spell out 6. Move one card to the bottom, saying, "S." Move a second card to the bottom, saying, "I." Turn the third card face up, saying, "X." The card is the 6. Place it face up on the table. In the same way, spell out the 5, the 1, and then the rest of the digits in the telephone number. As you spell out the number, lay the cards out in a row, just as they were laid out at the beginning.

Notes

Practice this with several telephone numbers. The procedure is actually quite easy to remember.

At first you may have some difficulty remembering that you must consider the number of letters in the spelling of the card, and not the value of the card itself. For example, you may think of a 3 as having a value of three, whereas *the word* actually contains five letters. A little practice will solve the problem.

The explanation is lengthy, but this is a very fast trick which captivates spectators. Repeat it at least twice.

NINE TO ONE

This trick was inspired by a Martin Gardner invention and a derivation by Robert Neale.

In your pocket you have a packet of nine cards. The suits are unimportant, so from the face of the packet to the top these are the values: 3, jack, ace, king, 7, 4, 2, jack, 8. Let's assume that you're using blue-backed cards. The sixth card from the bottom, the 4, will be *red-backed*.

Remove the packet from your pocket and turn it face up. Deal it out in three rows so that, as you look at them, the cards are laid out like this:

$$3 \quad J \quad A$$
$$K \quad 7 \quad 4$$
$$2 \quad J \quad 8$$

Ask Wayne to help out. "This will be a spelling test, Wayne—but a very easy one. We'll see if you can spell out the names of these cards. On the first letter, touch the card you choose to spell. Then you touch the card next to it or below it for the next letter. And so on. For instance, if you were spelling 'seven,' you might do it like this."

Touch the 7 and spell S-E-V-E-N, touching a different card for each letter in the spelling. You may touch the adjoining card on either side, or you may touch the card immediately above or below it. You may not, however, move diagonally. You may, in fact, go back the way you came and touch cards you've touched previously.

Demonstrate the spelling of seven at least twice. The second time, demonstrate how Wayne might retrace his steps and touch a card more than once.

"You may start on any card, and we'll see how many you can spell."

He spells out a card. Have him hold his finger on the one he lands on. "Let's get rid of the face cards. Which one should we turn down first?" Turn over whichever one he indicates. "This is going to get tough now, because you have to end up on a *face-up* card. Now turn over the card you landed on and then spell it out the same way as you did the first one. By the way, you can spell on a face-down card; you just can't *land* on one."

He starts with the card he landed on and spells out its value as he did before. Have him hold his finger on it. "We'd better get rid of another face card. Which one?" He tells you, and you turn it face down. Again he notes the card he landed on, turns it face down, and then spells it out.

"Now we'll get rid of that last face card," you say, turning it face down.

Wayne continues the spelling process until only one card remains face up.

"Congratulations, Wayne. You did it perfectly. Remember now, you had complete freedom of choice as to which cards you would spell and how you would spell them. And there's only one card that you chose not to spell."

Turn the remaining card—the 4—face down in place. The red back stands out among the blue-backed cards. "Well, no wonder. It doesn't fit in with all the rest."

Note

Why does this work? As I indicated, something of a mathematical principle is in operation. Cards can be spelled out in three, four, or five letters. Since some cards are spelled out with an odd number of letters and some with an even number of letters, all one needs to do is to place the cards so that the red-backed card can never be reached by the spelling procedure. The trouble is that three other cards cannot be reached, either. Therefore, place face cards in these positions and eliminate them as the trick proceeds.

Obviously, any three- or five-letter cards can be substituted for the ones I use in the layout.

UNEXPECTED REVERSALS

FAN OUT

Take any nine cards and spread them out in a face-down fan. Ask a spectator to pull out one card slightly, lift it up, and look at its name. Then your helper is to push the card back into the fan. Note the number of the card from the top of the packet. Say, "I'll mix the cards a bit." Now move cards from the top to the bottom, taking one, two, or three at a time. The object is to move the chosen card to the fifth position from the top, so you add 13 to the number of the chosen card from the top. If the original position was sixth from the top, you'd add 13 to this and move 19

ILLUS. 63

cards from the top to the bottom.

Spread out the cards in a fan once more. Remove the card at the far right, turn it face up, and insert it halfway in at the second position from the left (Illus. 63). As you turn over the card, say, "I'm not sure what your card is. It could be this, or not." Say something similar as you turn over succeeding cards. Remove

ILLUS. 64

the card now at the far right, turn it face up, and insert it halfway in at the fourth position from the left end. Continue with the next two cards on the right, so that every other card is face up, sticking halfway out of the deck (Illus. 64).

Close up the fan and turn the pile over edgewise, the cards still sticking out of the deck. Hold the packet with both hands. Your right hand from above grips its lower portion loosely. Your left hand from below grips the upper portion (Illus. 65). With your left first finger, push down the protruding cards so that they plunge out three cards below the packet (Illus. 66). Pull these cards away from the packet with your right hand. With your left thumb, flip over the packet remaining in your left hand. Drop the cards in your right hand onto this packet. Call attention to the face-up card, saying "It might be this card." Remove the face-down card from the back of the pile. Turn it face up, saying, "But I'm pretty sure it isn't this one." Drop it face up on the face of the packet. Flip the entire pile over, saying, "There's only one way I can find out for sure. What's the name of your card?"

ILLUS. 65

ILLUS. 66

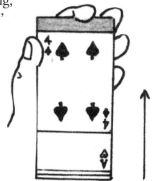

When the name is given, spread out the cards, showing the chosen card face up in the middle.

RIGHT HAND NOT SHOWN FOR CLARITY.

OVER & OVER

This trick requires no technical skill at all. Have someone cut the deck into two piles which are approximately even. Your

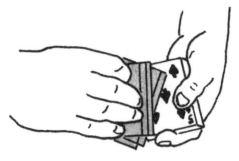

ILLUS. 67

volunteer is to look at the top card of one pile, and then turn the other pile face up on it.

Take the deck and fan off several cards. Turn them over endwise on the others, turning your right hand over in the process (Illus. 67). Push off several more cards with your left thumb. Take these under the cards in your right hand. Then turn your hand back to its original position. Add cards to the bottom each time, as you continue turning your hand over and back.

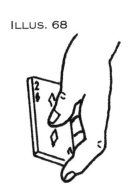

ILLUS. 68

When you get to the first face-down card (the chosen one), add it to the group you're currently fanning. Move your right hand away and flip over the cards in your left hand with your left thumb (Illus. 68). Bring your right hand back and add several cards from your left hand to the bottom of those in your right. Turn over your right hand and add cards to the bottom, as before. Continue until all the cards are in your right hand. Even up the cards.

The bottom portion of the deck is face up, and the top portion is face down. You may see a natural break between the two sections. If you don't, tilt the cards forward and riffle the inner edge with your right thumb until you find the break. Lift off the face-down cards with your right hand. Flip over the face-up cards with your left thumb. Place the portion that's in your right hand on top.

Ask the spectator to name the chosen card. It is the only face-up card in the face-down deck.

The sloppier you can make the shuffling, the better.

WHAT'S UP?

I came across this trick in Walter B. Gibson's 1947 book, *Professional Magic for Amateurs*. I do Gibson's version, with an improvement.

Ask Vernon to help out. Shuffle the deck and cut off about two thirds of the cards. "These are mine," you say. Hand Vernon the lower third, saying, "And the other half is for you." Turn away and continue: "Please shuffle your cards." You also shuffle yours. "Now we'll each choose a card from our pile. Kindly show your selection around and then hold it face down."

Turn away, note the bottom card of your pile, and turn it face up on the bottom. Turn over the entire pile, so that the card you looked at is the lone face-down card on top of the pile. Take any other card and hold it face down in your right hand.

Ask Vernon if he's ready. Turn back, saying, "I don't want to know your card, and I don't want you to know mine." Set the card that's in your hand on the table, telling him to do the same with his card. Pick up his card and carefully slide it into your pile, about two thirds of the way down. "Take my card and sneak it into your pile the same way."

Now you're holding all face-up cards with the exception of the top card, which you know, and the spectator's card, which you just stuck into your pile.

Casually drop your left hand to your side as you extravagantly gesture with your right hand and say, "Would you be good enough to give me your pile, please?"

You dropped your left hand with the palm up (Illus. 69). Bring your hand up with the palm *down*, back of the hand

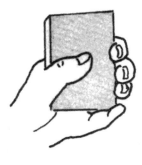

ILLUS. 69   ILLUS. 70

uppermost (Illus. 70). Place the spectator's pile below this pile and take the entire pack into your right hand.

"My card was…" Name the card you looked at earlier. "What was the name of your card?" Repeat the names of both cards. Then spread out the deck, revealing that both are face up.

RED & BLACK MAGIC

THE FORECAST IS FAIR

Arthur Hill developed this prediction trick; I've added some variations.

Cecilia volunteers to help out. After she shuffles the pack, fan through the cards, noting the first black card from the bottom. Suppose it's the 6 of clubs. Continue fanning through the cards until you come to its mate, the 6 of spades. Place this card face down on the table, saying, "Here's my prediction card."

Spread the deck face down on the table, saying, "Cecilia, I'd like you to take 25 cards from the deck. Take them in bunches, or singly—whatever you wish. So you'll be sure I won't know any of the cards, don't take from too near the top or the bottom." This instruction ensures that she doesn't take that first black card from the bottom. After she's taken her cards, have her check the count. "So now you have half the deck. Well, almost half the deck. I get the extra card. After all, it's *my* trick." Gather up the remaining spread-out cards, making sure that the first black card from the bottom stays in the same position. Set your packet on the table.

"The object of this trick is to show the close relationship between the red and the black cards in the deck. I'd like you to secretly count the number of red cards that you have."

When she finishes, have her set her packet on the table. Now do your best to thoroughly confuse the onlookers. Have Cecilia cut off some cards from her pile and shuffle them. She sets these down and shuffles the remainder of her original pile. She cuts off some cards from the top of *your* pile, shuffles them, and sets them next to your original pile. In other words, she shuffles both of her piles and the top portion of your original pile.

Gather up the cards. Her two piles go on the bottom. Your unshuffled portion goes on next, and your shuffled pile goes on top.

"Now we'll find out if there's actually a relationship between the red and black cards. How many red cards did you have?" Suppose she says 12. "Let's count down to that same number of black cards." From the face-down deck, deal the cards into a face-up pile, counting aloud as you come to each black card. When you come to the twelfth black card, toss it aside face up. Gather up the cards and set the deck aside. Finally, show that your prediction card matches the one that was counted to.

Stop Sign

Roy Walton invented this location trick based on a principle similar to that used in "The Forecast Is Fair," on page 150.

Ask Doug to shuffle the pack and then deal into a face-down pile. He must deal fewer than 26. Secretly keep track of the number he deals. Subtract this number from 27. This is your key number. Suppose he's dealt 18 cards. Subtract 18 from 27, giving you 9. You must remember the number nine.

Tell Doug, "Please pick up the cards you dealt off. Fan through them and secretly count the red cards." When he's done, turn away, and continue: "Set that pile down and pick up the rest of the deck. Now you counted a certain number of red cards. I want you to look at the faces and count to that same number in *black* cards. For instance, if you counted 12 red cards, you'd count to the twelfth black card from the bottom. That will be your selected card." When he's done, say, "Close up the cards and turn them face down. Place them on top of the pile on the table."

Turn back, pattering, "What we've tried to do is have a card selected completely at random. Now let's see if I can read your thoughts. Pick up the deck and slowly deal the cards, one by one, into a face-up pile. When you come to your card, I want you to *think* 'stop.' But try not to pause, hesitate, or in any way give away the position of your card. Just continue dealing at the same pace."

As he deals, count the black cards. The card that lies at your key number (in our example, the ninth black card) is the one he chose. Let him deal a card or two more and then say, "I got a strong impression a moment ago." Push the chosen card out from the others. "Is this your card?"

THE ONE & ONLY

The original trick is the invention of Karl Fulves. In its effect, it is somewhat similar to "Nine to One," on page 142, but the principle is totally different.

Let's assume you're using a deck with blue backs. You're going to use 16 cards, eight of the black suits and eight of the red suits. The values and the specific suits don't matter. One of the red-suit cards, however, will be from a different deck and will have a *red back*. Let's say this card is the queen of hearts.

Remove the packet of 16 cards from your pocket and turn it face up. Deal the cards out face up. This is how they'll appear from the spectator's view:

B	R	R	R
R	B	B	B
R	B	QH	R
R	B	B	B

So, for you to deal the packet out in a natural order—left to right, one row below another—the cards must be set up, from the bottom of the packet, like this: B B B R, R QH B R, B B B R, R R R B.

You'll also need a marker of some sort. A mysterious-looking medal or a foreign coin is perfect. Any coin will do, however. Hand the coin to a spectator, saying, "This will aid us in an experiment to determine whether our minds are in tune. If all works out, it might be an example of coincidence...or it might be some mysterious form of telepathy. I'll turn my back and give you some instructions. I want you to act on impulse only. Do whatever first occurs to you. If you stop to think, it could conceivably interfere with any possible telepathic waves."

Turn away and give the following instructions, pausing after each:

"Place the coin on any *red* card—complete freedom of choice."

"Move the coin to the left or the right to the nearest black card; you may choose *either* left or right. If there's no black card to the left or right, just leave the coin where it is."

"Move the coin either up or down to the nearest red card. Again, you have the choice of going *either* up or down."

"Move the coin diagonally to the nearest black card."

"Move the coin either down—towards you—or to the right to the nearest red card."

Turn back. The coin should be resting on the queen of hearts. "Let's see if we were able to mentally communicate." Turn over, in place, all of the cards except for the queen of hearts. "All blue backs." Remove the coin from the queen of hearts and turn the card over. It is, of course, the only card with a red back.

LONG-DISTANCE CALLS

PHONY COINCIDENCE

By way of preparation, write a column of numbers, from one to 35, on a sheet of paper. Phone Ramona and ask her to get a deck of cards.

"Please give the cards a good shuffle, Ramona. Now it happens that I'm thinking of a particular card. I wonder if *you'd* choose the same card. Let's find out. Cut off a pile of cards. Set the rest of the deck aside. Now from the top, deal your cards into a face-up pile. Please name each card as you deal it out. Keep going until you finish the pile you cut off."

As Ramona names each card, jot down that number next to the appropriate number on your sheet. (Use this shorthand: For 9 of clubs, 9C; for queens of spades, QS; for ace of hearts, AH, etc.)

When Ramona finishes naming the cards, say, "That's amazing! My card is in that group."

Your key numbers are 1, 2, 4, 8, 16, 32. Note how many cards are in Ramona's pile. *Subtract from this the next-lower key number.* Suppose the pile contained 23 cards. Subtract the next-lower key number, which is 16. Twenty-three minus 16 is 7. Double the result, which gives you 14. Look at your sheet. The card at number 14 will be the one you're thinking of.

Say to Ramona, "Pick up your pile and turn the cards face down. Now deal the top card onto the deck and put the next one on the bottom of your pile. Put the next one on top of the deck and the next one on the bottom of your pile. Keep doing this until you have only one card left."

When she's done, say, "The card I was thinking of was…" Name the card you noted at number 14. Ask, "What's your card?" It's the same, of course.

A brief review of the latter part of the trick: Your helper has finished listing her cards. You note the number in the pile.

Suppose the total is 14. You subtract from this the next-lower key number, which is 8. Fourteen minus 8 is six. You double 6, giving you 12. The card you noted at number 12 will be the one your helper will end up with.

ARE YOU THERE?

Have a pencil and paper ready. Phone a friend and ask him to get out a deck of cards. Give him the following directions:

"Shuffle the deck. Look at the bottom card and remember it. Count onto the table from the top of the deck a number equal to the value of the card you looked at. A jack counts as 11, a queen 12, and a king 13. Now place the rest of the deck on top of those cards."

When he's done, say, "Now name the cards, starting with the top card of the deck and working on down." After he names the first card, say, "Stop! I forgot something. Put that card back on top. I wanted you to cut the cards first. Cut off about half the cards and place the other half on top."

But make sure you jot down the name of the card he called out. This is your key card. After he cuts the cards, say, "Now please name the cards, starting with the top card."

As he names the cards, jot down their names, using this shorthand: AC, 9H, 2D, etc. Stop writing when the spectator calls the name of the key card. Suppose that card were the 9 of diamonds. These might be the last 15 cards you jotted down:

5D 2H 7H 10H 5H 9H JS 5C AC KD JC 8H 7S 4D 9D
13 12 11 10 9   8 7   6   5   4   3   2 1 — —

Now number the cards as above. Don't put a number under your key card, nor under the card named before it. When a number corresponds to the value of a listed card, that's the chosen card. In the example above, the chosen card is the 10 of hearts. If there are two possibilities, eliminate one by naming the suit or value of one of the cards. For instance, you might say, "I get a strong feeling that your card is a club." If your assistant agrees, you have the right card. If you're wrong, name the other possibility.

SOMETHING TO SNIFF AT

As far as I know, the original telephone trick was called *The Wizard*. Spread out the cards face up and have someone push out a card. Then dial "The Wizard," actually a confederate. When your friend answers the phone, ask, "Is The Wizard there?" Immediately the confederate begins naming the suits. Upon hearing the correct suit, you say, "Hello." Your confederate now knows the suit of the chosen card. She immediately begins naming the values, like this, "Ace, king, queen, jack, 10," etc. When she names the proper value, say, "Here," and hand the phone to the person who chose the card. The Wizard immediately tells him the name of his card.

Here we have an extremely subtle adaptation of the same trick. Again, the deck is spread out face up and a spectator pushes out a card. Dial the number of your confederate. When she answers, clear your throat. As before, she begins naming the suits. When she hits the correct suit, you sniff. She names the values. When she hits the right value, you again sniff.

Hand the phone to the spectator. Whisper to him, "Ask for your card any way you want to." When the spectator says "Hello," your confederate says, "Hello, hello. Who's calling, please? Hello." This, of course, creates the illusion that she's just answered the phone.

The spectator asks for the name of his card and is given the correct answer.

SPECIAL ARRANGEMENTS

EASY OPENER

Jay Ose often used this opening trick; I've made a few minor changes.

Remove the four aces from the deck. The ace of hearts goes on top of the deck, and the ace of diamonds goes on the bottom. The third card from the top is the ace of clubs, and the fourth card from the top is the ace of spades. Place the deck in its card case.

In performance, get a volunteer—Susie, for instance. Remove the deck from its case and set the case aside. Set the deck on the table. Make sure no one gets a peek at the bottom card.

"Susie, I'd like you to think of an ace—A-C-E, ace. It could be your favorite ace, or one you don't care for at all. Do you have an ace in mind? What is it?"

She names the ace. Suppose she names the ace of hearts. Say, "Put your hand on top of the deck and say, 'I want the top card to be the ace of hearts.'" She does so. Have her lift her hand. Turn over the top card, showing that her wish has come true.

Suppose she names the ace of diamonds. Say, "Put your hand on top of the deck and say, 'I want the bottom card to be the ace of diamonds.'" She removes her hand and you turn the deck over, showing the bottom card. Make sure that you don't inadvertently show the top card as well.

Suppose she names the ace of clubs or the ace of spades. Say, "As I said, 'Ace, A-C-E.'" Pick up the deck. Spell out A-C-E, dealing one card from the top into a pile for each letter. If she named the ace of clubs, turn over the last card you dealt. If she named the ace of spades, turn over the current top card of the deck.

In all instances, gather up the cards and give them a good

shuffle, destroying all the evidence. As you do so, patter about how incredible it is that she should have thought of that very ace. Go right into your next trick.

It's in Your Hands

The spectator handles the cards throughout an "impossible" location of a chosen card.

In preparation, remove all the clubs from the deck. From top to bottom, arrange them in this order:

10 9 8 7 6 5 4 3 2 A K Q J

The stack goes on the bottom of the deck, making the jack of clubs the bottom card.

In performance, set the deck face down on the table. Ask Bert to cut off a portion and shuffle it. Make sure he doesn't cut into your stack. "Replace the packet on top of the deck, please. Then take the top card, show it around, and replace it on the top."

When Bert's done, have him give the pack a complete cut. He, or someone else, gives the deck another complete cut.

Say, "Let's try something different. Turn the deck face up and give the cards a complete cut."

Have various spectators continue cutting the cards until a club shows up on the face of the deck. At this point, say, "That should be enough. The cards should be sufficiently mixed. Turn the deck face down, please."

You now know the position of the chosen card from the top. How? You add 3 to the value of the bottom card. Suppose a spectator has cut the 6 of clubs to the bottom. Add 3 to 6, getting 9. The chosen card is ninth from the top. The ace is figured as one.

The obvious exception is when the jack, queen, or king of

clubs is cut to the face of the deck. Just consider the jack as one, the queen as two, and the king as three—which should be easy to remember. So if the jack appears on the bottom, the chosen card will be on top; if the queen is on the bottom, the chosen card will be second from the top; and if it's the king, the chosen card will be third from the top.

As before, suppose the 6 of clubs was on the bottom. The deck is now face down on the table, and you know the chosen card is ninth from the top.

Harry Lorayne suggested this procedure: Have the spectator place his hand on the deck. Say, "Your card is forty-first from the top, so please push down on the deck. Good! It's now twenty-fifth from the top. Push down a little harder. Hold it, hold it! You now have it ninth from the top. Any more pushing and you might push it out of the deck altogether. Let's check that ninth card and see if I'm right."

Have the spectator deal off nine cards into a pile. Ask him to name his card and then to turn over the last one dealt.

Note

In the original version of this trick, the cards were stacked on the bottom in their natural order. This could give the trick away. A *five* shows up on the bottom, and the chosen card is *five* from the top. Not good.

FOUR OF A KIND

Milt Kort called my attention to this trick; I've made a few changes in the handling.

Here's the way you make the setup. Remove from the deck all threes, sixes, sevens, nines, and fives. Actually, any five values will do, but these seem to work well in keeping the setup concealed. Mixing the suits, make a set of five which includes all five values in random order. For example, place the 9 of clubs

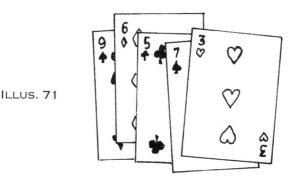

face up on the table. On top of it, face up, place the 6 of diamonds. Next, the 5 of clubs. Then the 7 of spades. Last, the 3 of
hearts. The suits don't matter so long as they're chosen ran-
domly. From bottom to top, you now have face up on the table
9, 6, 5, 7, 3, and the suits are mixed (Illus. 71).

On top of these, place face up another set of five in exactly
the same order, mixing the suits. Do this twice more. Pick up
your stack and put it face down on top of the deck. Put the
deck in its case, and you're ready to go.

To perform, remove the deck from the case. From the top
deal 20 cards into a pile on the table, counting aloud as you do
so. For our purposes, the setup is still retained. Set aside the rest
of the deck.

"This little experiment has its ups and downs," you say.
"Here, for example, I've dealt 20 cards *down*." Ask Johanna to
assist you. "Johanna, please give the cards a complete cut." After
she does so, have the cards cut at least once more—by Johanna,
or by someone else.

Say to Johanna, "I'd like you to put the cards behind your
back and give the packet a complete cut. As I mentioned, this
experiment has its ups and downs. What I'd like you to do is
turn the top card of your packet face up, and then cut the cards
again." When she's done, have her bring the packet forward.

Take the cards from her, saying. "Your card is now face up. Watch how I magically cause the card to turn face down." Turn the packet face up and fan through to her face-down card. "See! There it is. Not my best work, maybe, but it's a start." Set all the cards to the right of her card face up on the table. Place her card face down on the table in a position near you. Take the remaining cards into your right hand and drop them face up onto the face-up packet on the table. You've removed her card and have managed to cut the packet at the point where her reversed card lay.

"Now we're going to find out how lucky you are. We'll need to have two equal piles." Hold the cards face down in the dealing position in your left hand. Spread out the top two cards and take them in your right hand, saying, "Two." Take the next card *under* the cards in your right hand, saying, "Three." Take the next card the same way, saying, "Four." Repeat with the next card, saying, "Five." Drop these onto the table.

Do *precisely the same thing* with the next five cards, dropping them on top of the first five. "Five and five…that's ten," you say.

Now form a pile to the right of the first pile. This time the counting procedure will be similar, but different. Again take the top two cards, saying, "Two." Push off the next card and, with your right thumb, draw it *on top* of the two in your right hand. As you do so, say, "Three." Draw the next card on top of those in your right hand, saying, "Four." Repeat the procedure, saying, "Five." Drop these onto the table to the right of the pile of ten.

You have four cards remaining in your hand. Take the top two in your right hand, saying, "Two." Draw the next card on top of these with your right thumb, saying, "Three." Repeat the procedure, saying, "Four." Drop the four cards on top of the pile on the right. "Five and four make nine. That's close enough. Besides, that will give us a bonus card."

Push the two piles towards Johanna. "Now I'd like you to

turn over the top card of each packet to see if the two cards match in value." She turns over the two cards; they don't match. "No match. Well, life has its ups and downs." Take the two cards and set them aside *face down.* "Try again." Once more there's no match. Take these two cards and place them face down with the others. *Don't name the value of the cards as she turns them over.*

Have Johanna continue. When she turns over the fifth pair, she *has* a match. "A match! Excellent!" Take these two cards and set them, *face up,* near the card she originally reversed. "Now let's see if you can find any more matches." She continues with the next four pairs without success. In each instance, turn the cards face down and toss them into the discard pile. One card remains face down on the table. Point to it, saying, "And we have our bonus card."

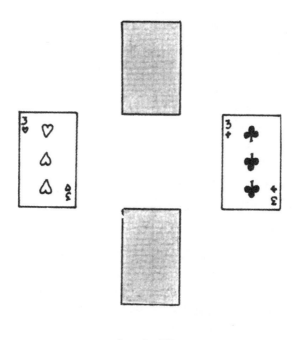

ILLUS. 72

At this point, for visual effect, I have the four cards in a diamond formation. Nearest to me is the originally reversed card. To the right and forward of it is one of the matched cards, face up. Forming the top point of the diamond is the "bonus card," which is face down. To the left and forward of the originally reversed card is the other matched card, face up (Illus. 72).

Turn over the two face-down cards. Say, "All four match! Johanna, you may have your ups and downs, but you're *extremely* lucky."

As you speak, gather up the unmatched pairs and shuffle them into the deck.

Note

You can use two different procedures in counting the 19 cards so that the unmatched pairs will have a maximum variety, thus allaying suspicion of a setup. You immediately turn the unmatched pairs face down so that spectators will be less likely to note the repetition of specific values.

Most Magicians

This routine was originally developed by Stewart James. I like to do the J. W. Sarles version.

A simple setup is required: In a face-up pile place any six spades, other than those used in the spade royal flush. On top of these, place the ace of clubs, ace of hearts, and ace of diamonds, in any order. On top of these, in order, place the ace of spades, 10 of spades, jack of spades, queen of spades, and king of spades. Place all on top of the deck.

Sidney will assist you. Explain, "Most magicians have a card selected like this. They either fan the cards out face down." Do so. "Or they fan the cards out face up." Do so, making sure you don't fan into your setup. "But I'm not most magicians." Close up the cards and turn them face down. Address Sidney: "I'd like you to give me a number between ten and 20." He gives you the number. You deal that many cards into a face-down pile onto the table.

Tap the last card dealt. "Most magicians would have you take this card. But I'm not most magicians." Set the rest of the deck aside for the moment. Pick up the pile you just dealt. Let's suppose Sidney chose the number 15. "You had me deal out 15 cards. The digits are 1 and 5. Let's add them together. What do we get?" He replies. "Right, 6." Deal six cards into a pile. Tap the last card you dealt and avert your head. "I'd like you to look at this card and show it around. Then replace it on top of the pile."

When he's done, place the pile in your hand on top of the pile on the table. Pick up the combined pile. "Let's mix these up a bit," you say. Remember the number Sidney chose? Now transfer that number of cards from the top to the bottom of the pile, moving one, two, or three cards each time. At the end of this "shuffle," the packet will be in precisely the same order. As you transfer cards, silently keep track. In our example, move 15 cards and then quit. "That should do it," you declare. Place the packet on top of the deck.

Spread out some of the top cards, saying, "Most magicians would fan through the deck and find your card. But..." At this point, you can either pantomime the rest of the statement, or let the audience complete it for you. Say, "Instead, I'm going to see if the deck will tell me what your card is." Hold the deck to your ear and thoughtfully riffle the edges. Gradually you reveal that the card is black, a spade, the ace of spades. For each revelation, give the cards a little riffle.

Bring the deck forward and give a satisfied smile. Spectators will assume you're done.

Continue: "*Most* magicians would consider that enough. But..." Pause a moment, pointing your thumbs towards yourself. "Your card is the ace of spades. Let's spell *ace*." Spell *ace*, putting into a pile one card for each letter in the spelling. "Now, *spades*." To the right of the first pile, spell out *spades* in the same way. Turn over the top card of the deck. It's the ace of spades. Set the ace of spades face up beyond the two piles on the table.

Again, smile and give a little nod, as though you're done. Pause. Then say, "*Most* magicians…" You need not say any more. Point to the three-card pile on the table. "Here we have the ace pile." Turn the cards over, showing the three aces. "And here we have the spades pile." Turn over the other pile, showing the six spades.

"Thank you, thank you," you say, taking a little bow. Pause.

"*Most* magicians…" Pause. "But we're not quite done," you say. "We have the ace of spades, and we'll require four more cards to make a poker hand." Deal off four cards from the top into a face-down pile. Now turn these cards over one by one, setting them in a row next to the ace of spades. As you do so, say, "*Most* magicians would quit right now. And so will I…because you can't beat a royal flush in spades."

CUTTING THE ACES

Wally Wilson dazzled me with this trick. I have no idea who originated the effect, which is a clever adaptation of an old principle.

A simple setup is necessary. Collect the four aces and arrange them, along with two other cards, like this: Place an ace face up on the table. On top of this place another ace face up. The next card—any card but an ace—is also face up. On this place any card but an ace *face down*. And, on top of all, two face-down aces. So, from the top down, you have three face-down cards (ace, ace, any card), followed by

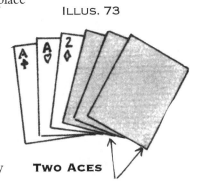

ILLUS. 73

TWO ACES

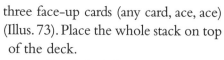

three face-up cards (any card, ace, ace) (Illus. 73). Place the whole stack on top of the deck.

Ready? Ask a spectator to help you. "As I riffle these cards, please stick your finger in wherever you wish." Hold the deck in the dealing position in your left hand. With your right fingers, riffle the outer end of the deck from the bottom up, going as slowly as you can (Illus.74).

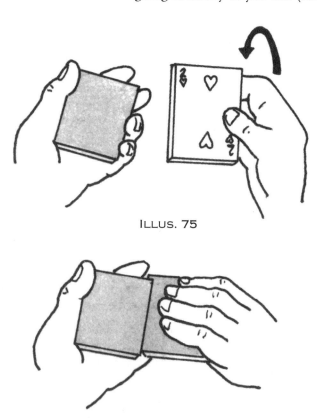

ILLUS. 75

After the spectator inserts his finger, lift off the upper portion with your right hand, allowing withdrawal of his finger. Turn this packet over sideways and place it face up onto the cards in your left hand, saying, "We'll mark the exact spot you chose."

Even up all the cards. Ask: "And where's the card you selected?" Fan through the pack to the first face-down card. Lift the face-up cards with your right hand. With your left thumb, push off the first face-down card so that it drops to the table, still face down.

Turn over the cards in your right hand *end for end* and place them beneath those in your left hand (Illus. 75).

Repeat the entire maneuver, starting with riffling the outer ends of the cards for the insertion of the spectator's finger. The business is performed four times in all.

At the end, you say, "Let's see which cards you selected." Turn the aces face up one by one.

Note

You'll end up with a face-up card in the deck. If you don't have an opportunity to secretly turn the card over, simply proceed with other tricks. What with various spectators shuffling the deck, it's not unusual that a card should turn out to be face up. When it's noticed, simply say, "No wonder I'm having so much trouble. We've got a face-up card here." Then turn the card over.

"Guts" Poker

U. F. Grant developed a brief poker demonstration. The demonstration should be done while seated at a table.

To start, you must have the four aces on top of the deck. Casually give the deck a few riffle-shuffles, keeping the four aces on top.

Explain, "Card sharps usually win, not by cheating, but because they know the odds. Sometimes they resort to cheating.

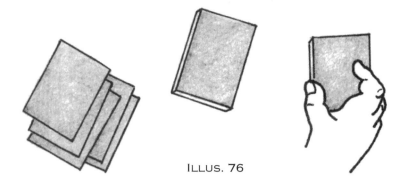

ILLUS. 76

But I've discovered that you don't have to know the odds and you don't have to cheat—*if* you're very lucky. And I happen to be very lucky. Let me demonstrate."

Ask Woody, who's seated opposite you, to help out. Set the deck down and ask the person seated to your right to cut the cards. After he picks a packet from the top, pick up the lower portion and begin dealing. This is a fairly normal procedure in informal games. The person who cut the cards will place his portion on the table.

Deal two poker hands in the normal manner—one to Woody and one to yourself. "This will be a wide-open game," you say. "You may draw as many cards as you want. But not more than five...if you don't mind."

You're still holding the packet you dealt from. "How many cards do you want?" He tosses some cards aside, and you deal him the same number. Then casually set the remaining cards down *to the right* of the other packet on the table (Illus. 76). Pick up your hand and study it, murmuring something like, "I seem to have run out of luck. This is the worst hand I've *ever* held." The point is to kill a little time, giving onlookers a chance to forget which packet is which. Finally discard four cards from your hand. "I guess I'll take four."

Pick up the pile which was originally the top section and deal yourself four cards—the aces, of course. Place the remaining cards on top of the packet on the table.

Do some imaginary betting with Woody, then ask him to show his hand. "As I mentioned, you don't have to be skillful—if you're lucky."

Turn over your cards one at a time.

ALL IN THE MIND

You might wonder why a trick this simple would work. After the deck is shuffled by a spectator, Ernie, take the cards back. Comment that you need a prediction card as you fan through the deck, faces towards yourself. At first, fan rapidly through the cards, noting the top card. Then fan through more slowly, looking for the mate to the top card—the one that matches it in color and value. Remove that card and set it aside, face down, announcing that it's your prediction.

Hand the deck face down to Ernie, saying, "Please deal the cards one at a time into a face-down pile." After he's dealt 15 cards or so, say, "You may stop any time you wish." When he stops, take the remainder of the cards from him and set them aside.

Tell him, "Pick up the pile you dealt and turn it face up. Now deal those into a *face-up* pile and stop whenever you wish." Again, when he stops, take the cards remaining in his hand and set them aside. Say, "Pick up the pile, turn it face down, and deal as many as you wish."

He stops; you take the remaining cards and set them aside. He continues, alternately dealing from a face-up packet and a face-down packet, until only one card remains. Take this card and set it next to your prediction card. If the card is face up, simply turn over your prediction card, showing the match. If the card is face down, turn over the two cards simultaneously.

Note

Make sure that the top card isn't an obvious one, like an ace or face card. On every other deal, the "chosen" card is briefly displayed, so it should be a spot card, which is unlikely to be noted. If the top card is an ace or face card, have a spectator give the cards an additional shuffle.

Good Companions

This trick was invented by Roy Walton. Openly remove ten matching pairs from the deck—that is, two nines, two threes, two fives, etc. Take only one pair of each value; for instance, don't take two pairs of nines. As you remove the pairs, place them in a face-up pile. Turn the pile face down. While removing the pairs, explain, "I'm removing ten pairs of matching cards to try an experiment. If it works, you'll see a demonstration of my mental powers. If not, you'll see a demonstration of my total humiliation."

Now perform a deceptive maneuver. In a casual overhand shuffle, draw off any *even* number of cards singly from the top. Drop the rest of the packet on top of these. You may repeat the maneuver a few times.

Deal the packet into two face-down piles, alternating the placement of the cards. Put one pile on top of the other. Now you'll need two assistants.

Give the cards a complete cut. Ask Alice to do the same. And ask Tony to also give the packet a complete cut. This makes three cuts in all, and three, of course, is a mystical number.

Deal the packet into two piles, alternating as before. Give one pile to Alice and the other to Tony.

Tell Alice, "Give your pile a complete cut. And you may give it another, if you wish. Now remove *either* the top or bottom card and, without looking at it, set it face down to one side." Give Tony the same instructions, only he sets his selection face down on top of Alice's card.

Address Alice again: "Please deal your remaining nine cards into a face-down row. You may deal from left to right or from right to left. You may deal with your packet face up or face down. But if you deal with the packet face up, deal the cards face down because I don't want to see any of the cards." If she decides to deal with the packet face up, avert your head while she deals.

Tony is given the same instructions, except that he is to deal his cards face down on top of Alice's cards. He may also start at either end and deal with the packet face up or face down.

When they're finished, you say, "Each of you selected a card completely at random. You cut your packet and selected either the top or bottom card. There's no way I could control your choice, right? And you had complete freedom in dealing out your cards in a row. Let's see what I can do."

Slowly pass your hand over the row of cards, trying to get a vibration. The second time you pass your hand over, it quivers a bit as you reach the center pair, but you continue on without pausing. Eventually, you'll choose the middle pair, the fifth pair from either end. Again you pass your hand over the row and your hand trembles visibly as it passes the middle pair. At length, you pass your hand very slowly over the cards and your hand trembles violently at the middle pair, so you drop it on top of these cards. "I get a strong vibration right here," you say. Turn over the pair, showing the cards and naming them. Turn over the originally selected pair. They are the exact mates to the ones you selected.

You can turn the other pairs face up as you gather them up. There's no evidence whatever of how you did it.

Lie Like a Rug

Jack Vosburgh invented this trick.

Before you begin, sneak a peek at the top card of the deck. Then you'll need the assistance of three spectators.

Set the deck on the table and ask one of the spectators to cut the cards into three piles. Each of the spectators now chooses a pile and takes the top card from it. Your job is to note which of the three takes the card that you know.

Explain, "This is an informal lie detector test. Over the years I've acquired the ability to tell if someone is lying. Let's test it out. In a moment, I'd like the three of you to decide which one of you will tell the truth about the card he selected. So *one* of you will be a truth-teller. The other two should name each other's card."

Make sure all is understood, then turn away while the three make their decision. When you turn back, ask each spectator in turn which card he took. Then point to one spectator, saying, "You're lying." Point to a second spectator and repeat the accusation. Point to the third spectator, saying, "Congratulations! *You* are a truth-teller."

How do you know? Simple. If the person who took the card you peeked at names that card, the other two are liars. If he names some other card, then he is one of the liars; the other liar is the one who names the card you peeked at.

HOPELESSLY LOST

There's apparently no way in the world a chosen card can be located. Yet you manage to find it.

Before you begin, peek at the top card and remember it; this is your key card. Fan the pack out face down and have Phyllis remove a group of cards from the middle. Set the rest of the deck down. Take the packet from Phyllis, saying, "I'd like you to *think* of one of these cards as I fan them out." Avert your head. "I won't watch your face." Of course you won't; you'll be too busy silently *counting* the cards as you slowly fan the faces of the cards for Phyllis's perusal.

After she's thought of one, hand her the packet. Turn away, saying, "Please remove your card and show it to everyone. Then place it face down on the table. Shuffle the rest of the packet and put that group on top of the deck. Now put your card on top."

You could continue giving directions with your back to the group. I usually find it best to turn back at this point to make sure my directions are followed exactly. Say, "Cut off about two thirds of the deck, please. Set that group on the table. Take the remaining third and give those cards a good shuffle. Place them on top of the deck. Obviously, your card is hopelessly lost. Still, give the deck a complete cut."

The pack may be given additional complete cuts. Take the deck and turn it face up. Continue: "Let's see if I can pick up your mental vibrations. I'll fan through the deck and, when you see your card, I'd like you to think the word *stop*. I won't watch your face because I don't want to get any physical signals." What a nice person you are! Of course the main reason you won't watch her face is that you'll be looking for your key card. When you see it, begin silently counting with the *next* card. Count the number that was in Phyllis's packet, and the last card you count is the one chosen.

Slow down as you near the end of the count, saying something like this: "I'm getting an exceptionally strong signal. Your card must be somewhere near. Perhaps I passed it. No! This is it, right here!"

PERFECTLY MENTAL

In many respects, this trick is a perfect demonstration of mind reading. A card is *freely* chosen and returned to the deck. The spectator immediately *shuffles* the deck. Nevertheless, the mentalist finds the card.

Every so often, the trick will misfire. If there is such a thing as telepathy, isn't it logical that occasionally the mentalist will get the wrong signal?

Start by getting a peek at the bottom card. This is your key card. You may give the pack a riffle shuffle, keeping the card on the bottom. Set the deck on the table and ask Leah to cut off a portion of the cards and set them on the table. Say, "Please take the card you cut to and show it around, but don't let me get a look at it." When she's done, point to the portion she cut off, saying, "Replace your card here and then put the rest of the deck on top." After she does so, say, "Now give the cards a good shuffle."

If she gives the deck one shuffle, say, "And another." Chances are, however, she'll give the cards two or three shuffles on her own. It doesn't matter whether she gives the pack riffle-shuffles, overhand shuffles, or a combination.

Take back the deck, saying, "I'd like you all to mentally picture the chosen card. Maybe this will help me discover which one it is." With an expression of deep concentration, fan through the cards, faces towards yourself. Watch for your key card. The one just preceding it is *probably* the chosen card. Tentatively pull this card from the deck, shaking your head. "I don't get *strong* vibrations, but this *might* be your card." Set the card face down on the table. Ask Leah to name her selection. If you get it right, nod, and turn the card over. If not, replace the card in the deck, saying, "Yes, I was afraid of that." Follow up with a sure-fire mental trick.

Notes

It's possible that the chosen card could be separated from your key card by one, two, or three cards. Some prefer asking probing questions to see if this is what's happened. When this is the case, the mentalist is often able to come up with the chosen card—eventually. I prefer the straightforward method, even though there's a minor risk of failure.

You can make this trick almost a certainty by using *two* easily remembered key cards, like the two black aces. Beforehand, for example, you might place the ace of clubs on top of the deck and the ace of spades on the bottom. Proceed as described above.

When you fan through the deck and find a single card between the two aces, you can be quite confident that's the one chosen. But suppose the black aces are separated. In all likelihood, the chosen card is the one preceding the ace of spades or the one after the ace of clubs. To discover which, ask a question to distinguish the two possibilities, like, "Was it a face card?" or "Was it a red card?" or "Did it have a very low value?"

As with the version using one key card, reveal your choice in a very tentative manner, leaving yourself an excuse for a possible failure.

Mystic Prediction

This is a Martin Gardner principle with a Henry Christ twist. This is my variation.

Have Don shuffle the deck. Take it back, saying, "I'll attempt to predict the future, so I'll need to find a card that will match one that you'll choose by chance."

Fan through the cards, faces towards yourself. Explain: "Notice that I don't change the position of any cards as I look for a good prediction." Note the *eighth* card from the bottom. Find its mate in the deck—that is, the card that matches it in value and color. For instance, if the eighth card from the bottom were the queen of clubs, you'd find the queen of spades. Remove this mate and place it face down on the table. Announce, "This is my prediction card." If the mate should be one of the first seven cards from the face of the deck, have the cards reshuffled. "No card stands out in my mind; maybe you should give them another shuffle," you say.

Hand the pack to Don. "We're going to have you choose a card using a random mathematical procedure. I'll describe the method that seems to work best for this experiment. Deal the top card of the deck face up, saying 'Ten' aloud. Then deal the next card face up on top of it, saying, 'Nine.' Continue down to one, or until you hit a match. Suppose you hit a 6 when you say 'Six' aloud. That would be a match, so you'd stop dealing in the pile. Then you'd begin another pile, again starting with ten. If you should get all the way down to one without a match, then you 'kill' that pile by placing a face-down card on top of it. In your counting, an ace is considered a one. And only tens count as ten; face cards don't.

"Undoubtedly you've heard that three, seven, or 13 are mystic numbers. True enough. But for precognition, *four* is the critical number. So we'll need exactly four piles."

Guide Don through the process. Each time he hits a match as he counts backwards from ten, have him stop and start a new pile. If he deals out ten cards without a match, have him place a card face down on the pile, "killing" it.

After he has dealt four piles, gather up the "dead" piles, turning over the top card of each so that all the cards face the same way. Have Don shuffle this packet of "dead" piles. He places the entire packet beneath the pile from which he's been dealing.

Don adds up the cards on the face of the remaining packets. For example, if two packets remain, and the last cards dealt on these packets were 9 and 7, you'd get 16. "You have 16. Please deal 16 cards into a face-down pile."

Take the last card he deals and, without looking at it, place it face down next to your prediction card. "Let's see if my prediction worked out. If it did, these two cards should match in value and color." Turn over the two simultaneously.

Notes

This trick is actually enhanced by a repetition or two.

In the unlikely event that all four piles are "dead," simply gather up all the cards and start the trick over from the beginning.

As mentioned, after the spectator has dealt four piles, gather up the "dead" piles, righting the top card of each. The spectator shuffles these together and places the stack *on the bottom* of the cards he has left. The reason: If you don't do this, a repetition will reveal that the chosen card is always eighth from the bottom.

THE BAMBOOZLER

Get a peek at the top card of the deck. Give the cards a riffle-shuffle, keeping it on top. Set the deck down on the table. Ask Megan to cut off a pile, gesturing to show that she is to place the top portion nearer herself. Tap the card which she cut to, saying, "This card will tell me…" Point to the top card of the pile nearer her, continuing, "…what that card is."

Lift off the card she cut to, look at it, *remember it*, and replace it. Make sure no one else can see its face. "Your card is—" Name the card you peeked at originally. Have her turn the card over. You're right, of course. *Toss this card aside face up.*

Place the packet nearer you on top of the other packet. Once more you know the top card of the deck and are ready for a repeat. But *not* until you blather for a moment.

"That always seems to work the first time I try it," you might say, "but the second time is almost impossible. But I have to try; otherwise, you might think it was mere coincidence."

Repeat the trick, again discarding the named card face up. Replace your pile on top of Megan's. Again you know the top card.

"This last time I'm going to attempt something even more difficult. I'm going to name *both* cards," you say.

Suppose the card now on top of the deck is the ace of clubs. Megan again cuts off a pile. Tap the card she cut to, saying, "This is the ace of clubs." Lift off the card and look at it. Suppose it's the 3 of hearts. Nod your head and say, "Good."

ILLUS. 77

Tap the top card of Megan's pile. "And this is the 3 of hearts." Lift the card off and hold it next to the actual 3 of hearts, making sure no one can see the faces of the cards (Illus. 77). "Oh-oh!" You appear disappointed as you see what the second card is. "I can't believe this."

Pause, shaking your head. "Ace of clubs and 3 of hearts." Take one of the cards into your right hand. Turn your hands over and simultaneously drop the two cards face up onto the table. This maneuver masks their original position in your hand.

Note

This trick is definitely a "quickie;" don't dawdle.

THE HOCUS-POCUS PAIRS

Remove from the deck all aces, kings, queens, jacks, and tens, placing the cards face up in a neat pile on the table. But don't remove the cards in their natural order. You want to create the notion that the selection is random. You might, for example, remove the cards in this order: 10, queen, ace, jack, and king. Remove another set of five cards to match these exactly. In other words, take out another 10, queen, ace, jack, and king. These are placed, one at a time, on top of the first set. When the packet is turned face down, the cards will be, from the top down, 10, queen, ace, jack, king, 10, queen, ace, jack, and king.

ILLUS. 78

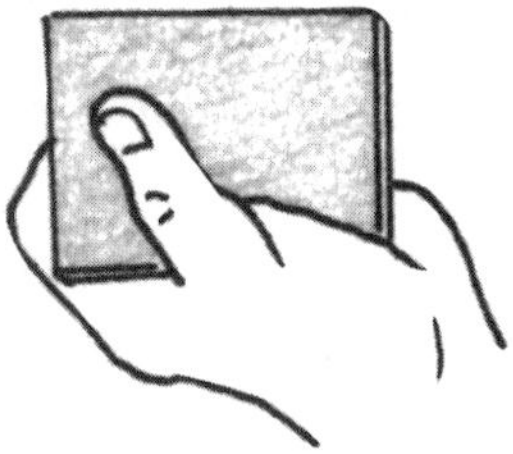

While doing this, explain, "I need fairly high cards for this experiment. Somehow or other, it always seems to work better with high cards. Maybe higher cards have more power."

Pick up the packet and turn it face down. Hold the cards in your left hand as though about to perform an overhand shuffle (Illus. 78). Lift some cards from the bottom with your right hand and drop these on top. Do this several times rapidly, as though shuffling. Actually, you're merely giving the packet complete cuts. The action should be performed casually as you continue chatting. Set the packet on the table and have spectators give it several complete cuts.

"We have ten cards here." Deal five cards into a pile, saying, "One, two, three, four, five." Fan out the remaining cards, saying, "And five more." Close up the fan and place this pile next to the other. You now have two piles on the table. One pile is in reverse order to the other. The first pile, for instance, might be in this order: ace, jack, king, 10, and queen. If so, the second pile will be in this order: queen, 10, king, jack, and ace.

Request Rosemary's help. "What brings about a miraculous result?" you ask. "The occult? Coincidence? We seldom know. Let's eliminate all but *two cards* and see if these two will match. We'll start by giving you a choice of two words which might bring about a miraculous result. An astonishing result might be caused by *telepathy* or *luck*. Choose one of those: *telepathy* or *luck*."

Rosemary selects one of the words.

Ask her: "Pick up either pile and spell that word, transferring one card from the top to the bottom for each letter in the spelling. You need not stick with one pile. You can spell a few from one and then a few from the other—any way you want to do it—just so you spell the word correctly."

When she's done, take the top card from each pile. Put them together and set them aside face down. "There. We've eliminated one pair. Now you have another choice to make. A miracle could be brought about through *ESP* or *fortune*. Choose one of those please."

After she chooses, have her spell out her choice, transferring cards from top to bottom, just as she did before. Again make it clear that she may switch piles at random as she does the spelling. When she finishes, set the top card of each pile aside as a pair, just as before. Say, "Another pair eliminated."

"You're now down to three cards in each pile. Time for

another choice. An apparent miracle might be caused by *magic* or by *accident*. Choose either *magic* or *accident*. Choose one and spell it out."

As before, when Rosemary finishes, set the top two cards aside as a pair.

"And again a choice. Is a miraculous result brought about by *sorcery* or *skill*? Please pick one and spell it out."

When she finishes, take the top two cards and set them aside as a pair, saying, "So we've eliminated the last pair. Only two cards are left. You've had several choices in eliminating the various pairs. Wouldn't it be an amazing coincidence if these two cards should match?"

Turn the two cards over, showing the match. Pause for a moment, as though through with the trick. "That may be coincidence, Rosemary, but let's see if you really have *the power*."

Turn over each of the other pairs, showing the other four matches.

Notes

For the trick to work, the exact words must be used each time. You might choose to carry a calling card on which you have the four pairs of words listed. At the appropriate time, take out the calling card, saying, "This experiment won't work unless we use the appropriate magical words." I prefer to have the "magical words" memorized.

PREDICTION PLUS

John Bannon came up with a great idea, and J. K. Hartman improved on it. My variation eliminates all sleights.

Have a spectator shuffle the deck. Take the cards back and start fanning through them, faces towards yourself. As you do so, note the bottom card. You're looking for the three cards of the same value.

"I need to make up a prediction packet," you explain. "So

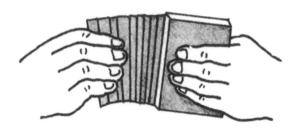

ILLUS. 79

I have to find three special cards." Suppose the bottom card is the 2 of hearts: you are seeking the other three twos. Very deliberately move the three twos, one by one, to the bottom of the deck. Naturally, you don't let anyone see the faces of the cards. Close up the deck. Then spread out five or six cards at the face of the deck. Nod your head and say, "All right."

Still keeping the cards facing you, place the tips of your right fingers beneath the fourth card from the bottom (Illus. 79). Look directly at the spectators and say with a smile, "I have my prediction; now someone else has to do some work." As you speak, close up the cards, picking off the four twos in a packet with your right hand. Make sure that the spectators don't see

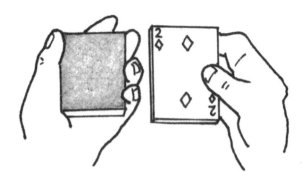

ILLUS. 80

the card on the face of the packet (Illus. 80). Immediately hand the deck to Oliver, saying, "Please shuffle the cards."

Through this next phase, continue holding your prediction packet exactly as you removed it from the deck—with its back to the spectators (Illus. 81).

When Oliver is sure the cards are thoroughly mixed, have him hold the deck face down and deal cards one at a time into a face-down pile. Tell him: "Stop whenever you wish." When he stops, say, "Are you sure you want to stop there? You may deal more if you wish." If he deals more, repeat the offer. When he's completely satisfied, have him place the packet in his hand next to the pile he dealt off.

Ask: "Could I possibly know the top card of either pile? If you think I could, please deal some more." He's satisfied at last. "Now your chosen card is the top card of one of these piles. Point to the pile you want."

Oliver points to one of the piles. Place your prediction pile *crosswise* on this pile (Illus. 82). "*This* is the pile you

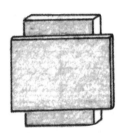

ILLUS. 82

chose." Immediately pick up the other pile and spread the cards out so that spectators can see the faces. Say, "You could have equally well chosen this pile and—as a matter of fact—any one of these cards." Set the pile aside.

"But you chose this pile." Pick up the pile with your right hand, casually aligning the prediction packet with the rest of the cards. Transfer the cards to the left hand. Deliberately deal off the top three cards, saying, "My prediction packet." Pause. Turn the next card face up, saying, "And your chosen card—the 2 of hearts." Toss it face up onto the table. Set aside the rest of the pile.

Pick up your prediction packet. One by one, turn over the other three twos, dealing them in a face-up row next to the chosen card.

Note

The timing in this trick is critical. Perform the trick exactly as described.

Prediction or Precognition

Staying Ahead

Quite common in mental magic is the "one ahead" principle. This trick, developed by Phil Goldstein, shows what powerful results can be obtained when it is used with subtlety.

You'll need a deck of cards, a pen, and two slips of paper of the exact same size.

Ask Herb to shuffle the deck. If you happen to get a glimpse of the bottom card, have him stop immediately and set the deck onto the table. If you don't get a peek at the bottom card, ask him to continue shuffling the cards. Still no peek? Have Herb hand the deck to another spectator. In the process, you may well get a peek. No? Ask the other spectator to shuffle. If you still don't get a look at the bottom card, go on to another trick.

But let's assume that Herb was kind enough to give you a peek at the bottom card and that the deck is now resting on the table. Look around for an empty ashtray or glass. Let's say you find a glass. Set it to one side on the table.

"I'll now make a prediction." On one slip of paper, print the name of the card you spotted. You might find it simplest to use the standard shorthand abbreviations for playing cards: 5H for the 5 of hearts, 6S for the 6 of spades, QD for the queen of diamonds, etc. Don't let anyone see what you're printing, of course. Fold the slip of paper twice, once down and once across. *Print* on the outside, in capital letters, *TWO*. Again, make sure no one can see what you're printing. Toss the folded slip into the glass. Spectators will probably not be able to read the number; nevertheless, try to toss the slip so that the printed side is down, and keep the glass a little distance from the group.

You'll need another assistant. "Betty, would you please cut the deck into two piles." She obliges.

"Now would you turn over the card you cut to and set it onto the table." She does so.

"Excellent! Now I'm going to try to make this experiment even more dramatic . . . if you can imagine such a thing."

Take the second slip of paper. Print on it the name of the card just chosen by Betty. Fold the slip of paper twice, as before, and print on the outside, in capital letters, *ONE*.

Toss this slip into the glass also.

"Now Betty, please pick up your face-up selection and place it on top of either pile—complete freedom of choice."

If Betty places the card on top of the pile which has your peeked-at card on the bottom, have her cut that pile. Then she is to place the other pile on top and give the whole deck a complete cut.

If she places the card on top of the pile she cut off, have her place the other pile on top and give the whole deck a complete cut.

In either instance, her card is somewhere in the deck, face to face with the card you glimpsed. Dump the slips from the glass onto the table.

"You chose a card, Betty; please name that card." She does. "Now will you open slip number one and read what it says." She reads off the name of her selection.

Turn to Herb. "Please take the deck from Betty and fan down to the face-up card. When you get to that card, please remove from the deck the card that faces it." He does. "What's the name of that card, Herb?" He names it. "Now please open up my second prediction and read what I have there." Sure enough, you're right again.

Notes

1) When you are putting information on the slips, make sure that no one sees exactly what you're writing. But don't be furtive about it. Instead, be smilingly casual.

2) Why do you print the numbers on the folded slips instead of using the numerals? Because spectators might notice the difference between the numerals one and two as you print them. This is unlikely to happen when you spell out the numbers.

ELIMINATE THE NEGATIVE

Hugh Nightingale developed an extremely clever trick that required a slight setup and a calculator. Using the basic idea, I came up with a totally impromptu trick.

June agrees to assist you, so ask her to give the deck a good shuffle. You take the cards back, saying, "Now I need to make a prediction." Fan through the cards, faces toward yourself. Note the top and bottom cards. Based on these two cards, you will select *two* cards as your prediction. One card will match the top card in value and the bottom card in suit. The other will match the *bottom* card in value and the top card in suit. Suppose the 9 of clubs is on top and the queen of hearts is on the bottom. You will remove from the deck these two cards: the 9 of hearts and the queen of clubs.

Set the two cards aside face down, saying, "These are my prediction cards. If all goes well, they will correctly predict our chosen card."

At this point, if you wish, you can give the deck a riffle shuffle. Just make sure you do not change the position of the top and bottom cards.

"June, we're now going to choose a card together. In the process, we'll discover whether our minds are on the same wavelength. To start, please cut the deck into two piles."

Let her create the two piles. Then, place your right hand over one pile and your left hand over the other. "Which one shall we eliminate?"

Now, she chooses one of the piles, and you place it to the side. If she chose the original top portion of the deck, you know that you must keep track of *the bottom card* of the other portion. If she chose the bottom portion, then you must keep track of *the top card* of the other portion. In other words, you keep track of the original top card or the original bottom card, depending on which pile was discarded. We'll call this card the *key card*.

"June, would you cut the remaining cards into two piles and hold your hands above them the way that I did." She does so. "Now I'll choose a pile to eliminate."

Obviously, you choose the pile that does not contain the key card. Have her set this pile aside with the other discarded pile.

"To speed things up, how about dealing the remaining cards into five piles. Deal them out just as though you were dealing hands in a card game."

Again, keep track of the key card.

"Now I'll hold my hands over two piles, and you choose the one to eliminate." Naturally, you hold your hands over two piles other than the one containing the key card. June sets aside the pile you choose.

Four piles remain. June holds her hands over two of these. You choose a pile other than the one containing the key card. This pile is discarded.

Three piles remain. You hold your hands over the two that do not contain the key card. June chooses one, and it is set aside.

Two piles remain. June holds her hands over them. You choose the one that does not contain the key card, and that pile is discarded.

Remaining is one small pile. "Let's see what card we chose between us." The key card is either on top or the bottom of this last pile. So, to display the key card, you either turn the pile face up or turn over the top card of the pile. In either instance, you announce the name of the card. "Ah, the queen of hearts!" you might say.

Turn over one of the prediction cards to see whether it's the suit or the value card. Let's say the card you turn over is the queen of clubs. You say, "And here we have a card which fore-told the value . . . a queen. And we also have a card which fore-told the suit . . ." Turn over the other card. ". . . a heart. The queen of hearts!"

Notes

1) As you fan through the deck to see what the top and bot-tom cards are, you might find that they are of the same suit or value. Just say, "I don't think these cards are mixed enough," and have the deck reshuffled.

2) Quite often when you have eliminated all but one pile, that pile will contain exactly three cards. You can deal these out in a row and continue the elimination. You hold your hands over the two piles that do not contain the key card. And then June holds her hands over the two remaining piles, and you choose the one that does not contain the key card.

3) The principle used in this trick is well known among magi-cians and has been used frequently in tricks with coins, poker chips, and other small objects. Years ago, I invented a version using cards. Until I came across this trick, I didn't know of any other adaptation of the principle to cards. You'll see my use of the principle in the next trick.

WORKING TOGETHER

Here I present two versions of the same powerful trick. Incidentally, I'd recommend that you not do this trick and the previous one in the same set for the same group.

Version 1: After Louis has shuffled the deck, fan through the cards, faces toward yourself. "I'm looking for a prediction card," you declare. Note the top card and remove from the deck its mate—that is, the card that matches it in color and value.

Without letting the spectators see this card, set it aside face down. "Here's my prediction."

Turn the deck face down and start dealing the cards into a pile, one at a time. After you have dealt ten cards, say to Louis, "Whenever you wish, tell me to stop." Continue to count the cards to yourself. When Louis tells you to stop, set the rest of the deck aside. Even up the cards you dealt off and hand them to Louis. "We're going to choose a card together, Louis. But first, let's lay out the cards. Just deal them out one at a time anywhere on the table."

Pay no particular attention as he lays out the cards at random. When he nears the end of the deal, you'd *better* pay attention, because you must know where the last card goes. This is the card that was originally on top of the deck—the *key card*—and you must keep track of it during the following.

You will now follow a procedure similar to that of the previous trick. You'll cover two cards with your hands (neither of which is the key card), and Louis will choose one to discard. Louis will cover two cards with his hands, and you'll choose one (not the key card) to discard. Eventually, only one card will remain on the table—the match for your prediction card. Hold this card face down. With your other hand, hold the prediction card face down next to it.

"Let's see if my prediction is correct," you say. Turn over both cards simultaneously. Shazam!

It's quite important that you count the number of cards you deal out. If the number is odd, the spectator gets first pick—that is, you cover two cards and the spectator picks. If the number is even, you pick first. Don't get this wrong, or the spectator will get the last pick. It's easy to know when the spectator picks first; just remember this: "The spectator is odd."

Version 2: This variation is sort of a "sucker trick."
Ask Jill's assistance. Tell her, "I'm sure that, working together,

we can end up with a very significant card." Continue chatting as you turn the deck face toward you and begin fanning through from the top. Note the color of the top card. Let's assume that it's a black card. Now you want to have 15 to 20 red cards below it, so you start taking out black cards from near the top and tossing them face down onto the table. "We'll start by eliminating some of these useless cards."

Continue removing the black cards until you have the desired setup. Push the black cards on the table to one side. Turn the cards in your hand face down. You should have one black card on top, followed by 15 to 20 red cards, and then the remainder of the deck.

Slowly deal seven or eight cards into a face-down pile. Then say to Jill, "Just tell me when to stop." Continue dealing slowly; she should stop you before you run out of red cards. As before, make sure you remember the number you deal out. Set the rest of the cards in your hand aside with the black cards you pushed aside previously.

Point to the cards you dealt out. "Jill, I'd like you to pick up that pile and deal them out, face down, all over the table. Place them wherever you wish." Jill distributes the cards face down onto the table; you make sure you see where she puts the last card.

"Ready, Jill? Now let's see if we can choose a truly significant card. We're going to take turns eliminating cards now. As each card is eliminated, I'd like you to keep it in a separate pile right in front of you."

Complete the selection of a card as in the previous version. Remember: If the number of cards on the table is odd, the spectator selects first; if the number is even, you select first.

At last, only one card is left. Point to it. "There it is, our significant card." Turn it over. Regardless of its value, rave about its significance. "I just knew this would be the card. What card could possibly be better? This particular card has a tremendous historical significance. And if I could remember what it is, you'd be absolutely thrilled." Somewhere along the line, someone should indicate some degree of dissatisfaction. If not, say, "I can see you're not particularly impressed. Turn over the cards we didn't pick, Jill." She does. "So Jill and I picked out the only black card. If that isn't significant, what is?"

Note

As you deal the cards into a pile, you ask Jill to tell you when to stop. But she shows no sign of stopping you, and you're almost out of red cards. "Sorry, Jill. I guess I didn't make myself clear." Pick up most of the red cards and place them back on top of those in your hand. Turn to someone else and say, "Would you please tell me when to stop."

THE RED ONE

Here we have a "packet trick." This means that you have a small number of cards in an envelope or wallet. These may be trick cards of some sort, or they may simply be cards that you don't ordinarily find in a deck—six jokers and two aces, for instance. The point is that you take these cards out and perform a wondrous trick.

Your packet, in this instance, consists of six cards. You'll be happy to know that these are not "trick cards" in any way. But neither are they ordinary.

ILLUS. 83

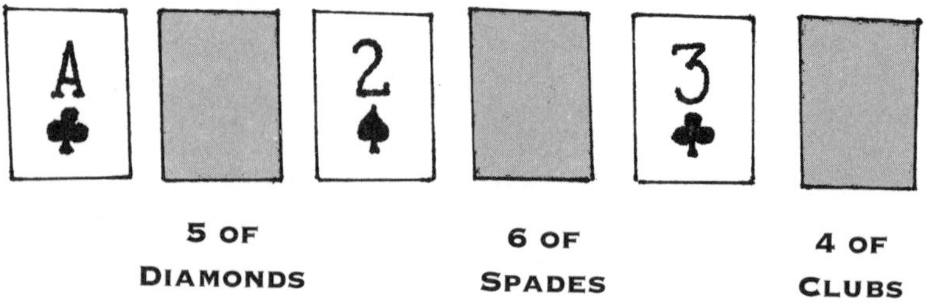

| 5 OF DIAMONDS | | 6 OF SPADES | | 4 OF CLUBS |

So you have six cards. Five are black spot cards (clubs or spades); one is a red spot card (heart or diamond). One of the black spot cards has a red back; all the other cards have a blue back.

Ultimately, the cards will be laid out as in Illus. 83. A spectator will be forced to choose either the second card or third card from your left. In our example, the face-down 5 of diamonds (the only red-faced card) is second from the left, and the face-up 2 of spades (the only red-backed card) is third from the left. In either instance, you'll demonstrate that the card selected is the only one different from the rest.

If the 5 of diamonds is chosen, you will turn over the other face-down cards. All the cards are now face up except for the 5 of diamonds. You point out that all the other cards are black. Turn over the 5 of diamonds; it's the only red-faced card.

If the 2 of spades is chosen, you will turn over the other face-up cards. All the cards are now face down except for the 2 of spades. You point out that all the other cards have blue backs. Turn over the 2 of spades; it's the only red-backed card.

Thus, it *appears* that the spectator chose the only card that's different from the others. Now let's see how precisely we arrive at this delightful conclusion.

Prior to your performance, set up the cards so that on top is the only red-faced card—in our example, the 5 of diamonds. Second from the bottom is the only red-backed card—in our example, the 2 of spades. (In our example, the setup, from top to bottom, will be 5 of diamonds, 6 of spades, 4 of clubs, 3 of clubs, 2 of spades, ace of clubs.)

In performance, get the assistance of Albert, who—poor boy!—actually thinks he has some degree of psychic ability.

"I'd like you to assist me in an experiment, Albert." Take the packet from your envelope, or wallet, or pocket. "I have six cards here. I'll send you a psychic message and see if you receive it."

Turn the packet face up and hold it in the left hand in the dealing position (Illus. 84).

In the illustration, the card at the face of the packet is the ace of clubs. Deal this card face up to your left. About four inches to the right of this, deal the next card (2 of spades) face up.

And, about four inches to the right of this, deal the next card (3 of clubs) face up (Illus. 85).

Turn the remaining three-card packet over. You're now holding the packet face down in your left hand in the dealing position. Deal the top card (5 of diamonds) face down into the first space on your left—in other words, between the face-up ace of clubs and 2 of spades. The next card (6 of spades) goes face down into the next space to the right, between the 2 of spades and 3 of clubs. And the last card (4 of clubs) goes face down on the right end. The cards are now in the position that was originally shown in Illus. 83.

"Six cards here, Albert, and I'm going to send you a psychic message." With fingers to temples, concentrate, hoping that Albert gets the message. "Now, Albert, please think of a number between one and six. After you've thought of one, change your mind, so that we'll know that this is not psychological. Do you have a number between one and six?"

ORIGINAL POSITIONS

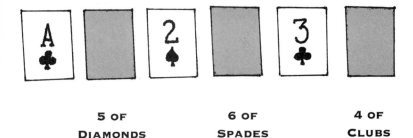

5 OF DIAMONDS   **6 OF SPADES**   **4 OF CLUBS**

He does. "Tell me the number, and we'll count it from the end."

Because you said "between one and six," he is confined to numbers two, three, four, or five. This means that Albert will end up with either the second or third card from your left. (Take a look at the original positions again, shown above.)

If he gives the number two or five, he will end up with the second card from your left. Say he gives the number two. Start with the card on the left end and count one, two—ending on the second card from your left. If he gives the number five, start with the card on the right end and count one, two, three, four, five—again ending on the second card from your left. In either instance, push the "chosen" card forward about an inch or so (Illus. 86).

ILLUS. 86

Turn the other face-down cards face up (Illus. 87). "Notice that all the others are black cards."

Turn over the "chosen" card. "And you picked the only red card of the group. Albert, you really are psychic." Gather up the cards and put them away.

If Albert gives the number three or four, he will end up with the third card from your left. Suppose he gives the number three. Start with the card on the left end and count one, two, three—ending on the third card from your left. If he gives the number four, start with the card on the right end and count one, two, three, four—again ending on the third card from your left. In either instance, push the "chosen" card forward an inch or so (Illus. 88).

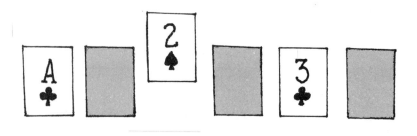

ILLUS. 88

Turn the other two face-up cards face down (Illus. 89).

"Notice that all the other cards have blue backs." Turn over the "chosen" card. "And you picked the only card in the group with a red back. Albert, you really are psychic."

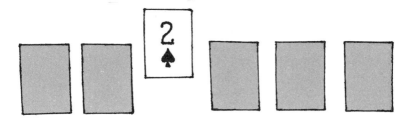

ILLUS. 89

Notes

1) It's easy to set up the cards so that you can perform immediately for another group. At the conclusion of the trick the six cards will either all be face up or face down. Simply gather them up so that the card that's second from the left becomes the top card (when the packet is face down) and the card that's third from the left becomes second from the bottom (also when the packet is face down).

2) When you ask the spectator to choose a number between one and six, he might just choose one or six. If he does, say, "I said 'between one and six.'" Have him choose another number. It's *your* trick; you can make whatever rules you wish. When this occurs (which is very seldom), the trick loses a little, but is still effective.

You might prefer this approach, however: Just spell O–N–E or S–I–X from the left. After all, if the spectator is not sharp enough to know what 'between' means, he's probably forgotten that you said you'd *count* from the end, and he's probably also forgotten his middle name.

It's Well-Suited

Richard Stride, adapting a principle developed by Paul Curry, invented a superb mental trick in which he makes use of business cards. My version uses a deck of playing cards and requires no preparation.

"I'd like you all to help me in an experiment," you explain. "We'll test how much psychic power this entire group has." As you continue chatting about psychic power, ESP, and mental waves, fan through the deck, faces toward yourself, and remove all the cards of one suit—clubs, for instance. Toss the cards face up onto the table.

"I have all the clubs here."

Hand the deck to Loretta, saying, "I'd appreciate it if you'd take all the hearts out of the deck and toss them onto the table. While you're doing that, I'm going to put the clubs in a secret and mystical order."

She takes out the hearts and you put the clubs in the mystical order which I will explain later. Set the clubs face down to one side and pick up the hearts.

"Let's see if you got them all," you say.

Put the ace of hearts face up on the table. On top of it place the 2 of hearts face up. And then the 3 of hearts face up. Continue all the way up through the king of hearts. As you place each card down, announce its value. Pick up the pile and turn it face down.

"Let me show you how we're going to mix this pile of hearts." Push off the top card of the packet (ace of hearts) with your left thumb and take the card into your right hand (Illus. 90).

ILLUS. 90

Push off the next card (2 of hearts) and slide the ace of hearts beneath it (Illus. 91).

Pick up both cards together, turn them face up, and set them face up onto the table so that they overlap somewhat (Illus. 92).

ILLUS. 92

"So sometimes I will mix two cards like this, and sometimes I'll just take one card." Push off the next card of the packet (3 of hearts), turn it face up, and set it face up on top of the two cards on the table.

Take two cards from the top of the deck, as described above, and place them face up on top of the face-up pile. As you do so, say, "Two." Then deal one card face up on top of the pile, saying, "One." Continue alternating like this until you come to the last two cards. The queen will be placed down singly, and so will the king.

If the cards were face down at this point, this would be their order from top to bottom:

2 Ace 3 5 4 6 8 7 9 Jack 10 Queen King

Pick up the pile from the table and fan the cards out so that all can see that they no longer retain their original order.

As you can see, the cards are fairly well mixed. Take the king of hearts from the bottom and toss it onto the table, still face up. Turn the packet face down. Pick up the king of hearts and place it face up on top of the packet.

"Very few people know what I'm about to tell you. In fact, I hardly know it myself. You see, the king of hearts is the master of all the cards. So let's see if he'll use his mysterious power over the other cards. We'll cut this packet several times, making sure that the king of hearts gets a chance to work through the packet."

Have three different spectators give the packet a complete cut. If the king is not somewhere in the middle of the packet, have the packet cut again.

"The first time, *I* mixed the cards. Now let's give other persons a chance . . . with the cards face down."

Hold the packet face down in the dealing position in your left hand.

"Let's start with you, Loretta. Shall we start with one or two cards?" If she says two, take the top card into your right hand and slide it under the next card, as before. Lift off the two and place them *face down* onto the table. If she says one, take off one card and place it *face down* onto the table.

Ask another spectator: "One or two?" Add to the pile according to that person's response. Continue with other spectators until the entire packet has been dealt face down.

It would seem that the packet would be quite mixed. As you'll see, it's not.

Pick up the packet and fan through it until you get to the face-up king of hearts. With your right hand, lift off all the cards above the king (Illus. 93). Set these cards onto the table.

"So we have the king of hearts in the middle."

Bring your right hand back to the remainder of the packet,

lift off the king of hearts, and then toss it, still face up, onto the table.

You address the group: "I wonder if I could ask you a favor." As you say this, with your right hand take the cards from your left hand and drop them face down onto the cards you just placed onto the table.

"Will it be all right if I put the king of hearts on top? You see, I'm going to try to match some of your cards with my prediction pile." Point to the clubs that you set up at the beginning. "And if I put your king of hearts on top . . ." Tap the king of hearts. ". . . then I know I'll get at least one card right."

Whether they agree or not, set the packet down and put the king of hearts on top, face down.

The heart packet now matches the club packet card for card. Let's complete the trick, and then I'll explain how this miracle came to be.

Set the club packet just to the right of the heart packet.

You now proceed to deny any responsibility for the outcome of the trick: "As you recall, I put the clubs in a secret and mystical order. But I take no responsibility for whether this works. You people cut the cards, and you people decided how to mix the packet. So if we don't match any other cards, it's all your fault."

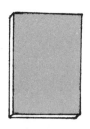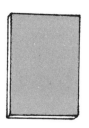

ILLUS. 94

Simultaneously turn over the top card of both piles. Naturally, they are both kings.

Smile proudly. "See? The one that I'm responsible for matches perfectly." Turn the kings face down. Set the king of clubs to the right of its packet and the king of hearts to the left of its packet (Illus. 94).

Turn over the top card of both piles. "Hey, you guys got a match!" Turn the cards face down and place them on top of the first discards.

Continue in the same way through all the other cards. As you go along, you show increased pleasure and surprise. After about five or six matches, your attitude has changed from total skepticism to proud assurance. "I knew you could do it. You've really got the power." And, at the end, you add this lie, which no one believes: "Unbelievable! This group got them all right. In all the years I've been doing this experiment, this is the first time this has ever happened."

How does it work? When you demonstrated that "one-or-two" shuffle, placing the cards down face up, the packet indeed became somewhat mixed. But when you did that same shuffle placing the cards face down, you simply reversed the order of the packet.

What about the cuts? Window dressing. You turned the king of hearts face up and let several spectators cut the cards. But complete cuts don't change the basic order of a sequence of cards. You then performed the "one-or-two" ritual, which reversed the order of the cards. And when you fanned through the packet to the king of hearts, you cut the cards at that point, which restored the packet to its proper order.

In the beginning, after you demonstrated the "one-or-two" technique, this was the order:

2 Ace 3 5 4 6 8 7 9 Jack 10 Queen King

Then the cards were cut several times, and you performed the "one-or-two" method with the cards face down. You, in effect, cut the king to the top, yielding this order:

King Queen 10 Jack 9 7 8 6 4 5 3 Ace 2

Note that this is the precise reverse of the other order. And this is the order in which you must arrange your "prediction pile," the clubs. The setup is quite easy to do. Fan the cards out, faces toward yourself. You are now going to place the cards face down onto the table, one at a time. As you do so, you'll consider them as several groups of three:

Ace 2 3 / 4 5 6 / 7 8 9 / 10 Jack Queen / King

The first group is ace, 2, 3, or 1, 2, 3. Place the middle card (2) face down onto the table, followed by the first card (ace) and the third card (3).

You do the same with the second group, 4, 5, 6. On top of the pile goes the middle card (5), followed by the first card (4), and then the third card (6). You follow the same procedure with the triplets 7, 8, 9, and 10, jack, queen. The king goes face down on top of all. Your "prediction pile" is ready.

And here is the order (from the bottom up):

2 Ace 3 / 5 4 6 / 8 7 9 / Jack 10 Queen / King

THE AMAZING TV TRICK

Watching a late show on TV one evening, I saw a famous mentalist perform a spectacular prediction trick. First, the mentalist set that day's copy of a newspaper on the table. Then he presented two decks of cards. He fanned through both, showing that they were ordinary in every way. The host of the show and his sidekick each chose a card from a different deck—with the cards in their own hands! Miraculously, both had chosen the same card. In the personals section of the newspaper was a prediction that they would choose the same card. What's more, the correct card was named. How amazing can you get!

Actually, the trick is quite easy. As with many effects, the presentation is key. If you want to do the trick on a formal occasion, you can take out an ad in the local newspaper for the day of the performance. The contents of the ad should be something like this:

"During the performance on (date), two persons will choose the same card—the 6 of clubs." Show the newspaper, saying, "I have taken out an ad in the 'Personals' section of this newspaper. We'll take a look at it later." Place the newspaper down in plain sight.

If you prefer, you can make the trick impromptu. Simply announce to the group that you'll make a prediction. On a slip of paper, write, "You'll both choose the 6 of clubs." Place the slip down in plain sight, or have a spectator hold it.

You want to make sure the audience knows that you're not using confederates. A good way is to have the group choose someone by consensus and then have this person select two persons to help you.

Produce two decks of cards. Hand one to each of your assistants, asking them to give the cards a good shuffle. Take the deck back from Jane. Hold the deck face up in the dealing position. Start fanning through the cards so that all can see the faces (Illus. 95).

ILLUS. 95

"Notice that the cards are ordinary in every way." After fanning several cards into your right hand, place these on top of the deck.

Fan through several more and place these on top also. Continue doing this until you come to the 6 of clubs, which you fan into the right hand below the others that you have already fanned over. Place this group on top of the deck. The 6 of clubs is now on top of the deck. Fan out several more cards, however. Then close up the deck, turn it face down, and set it on the table in front of Jane.

Take the deck from Jack and go through the precise same procedure as you did with the other deck. Set the deck on the table in front of Jack. The 6 of clubs, of course, is the top card.

"Now I would like each of you to pick up your deck. Please cut off a small packet of cards from the top, turn the packet over, and place it back on top of the deck." When they're done, continue, "Next, cut off a larger packet from the top of the deck, turn this packet over, and place it back on top of the deck."

Make sure they are following your instructions exactly. "Please, each of you fan off the face-up cards and set them down on the table. The next card in your pile will be your chosen card. But please don't look at it just yet."

Why shouldn't they look at it immediately? One reason is

that you want to build suspense. But more important, you want to give everyone a chance to forget exactly what happened. This is called "time misdirection." Given a chance, many spectators will forget that you even handled the cards, or that you carefully directed the choice of a card.

"Each of my assistants has selected a card completely at random. I doubt that anyone here could, with any confidence, name either chosen card. And don't forget that we have a newspaper right here, and that I took out a significant ad in it." Or, the last sentence might be, "And don't forget that I wrote something down on a slip of paper which has been in plain sight from the beginning."

Ask Jane to turn over the top card of those remaining in her hand. "What's the name of your card, please?"

She names it—the 6 of clubs. Do the same thing with Jack. Unbelievably, they both have selected the same card! And, even more incredibly, you have predicted their choice with an ad or by jotting the name on a slip of paper.

Note

If it doesn't strike you as too much trouble, you could use new, unopened decks. Unless you're doing a platform presentation, I think this might be a bit cumbersome, however. At someone's home, I highly recommend that, if possible, you borrow the two decks.

SIMPLE MULTIPLICATION

Of the general public, hardly anyone is familiar with this mathematical peculiarity: The number 142,857, when multiplied by 2, 3, 4, 5, or 6, will yield precisely the same digits that make up the original number. (In fact, the digits remain in the same basic order, which is not relevant in this trick.)

Some rudimentary tricks have been fashioned from this

principle. It seemed to me, however, that an excellent mental trick could be created. This one works quite well for me.

The only thing you need remember is the number I mentioned: 142,857. I use this mnemonic:

Unfortunate 57, as in 57 varieties. For purposes of the mnemonic, I pronounce "unfortunate" like this:

$$
\begin{array}{ll}
\text{un–} & (1) \\
\text{for–} & (4) \\
\text{tune–} & (2) \\
\text{ate.} & (8)
\end{array}
$$

So you get 1 (an ace), 4, 2, 8—and then 57 (varieties). As you can see, *142,857* is your key number.

To begin, ask George to assist you.

Fan through the deck, faces toward yourself, and remove cards that match your key number—except for the first digit. In other words, remove from the deck and place face down onto the table cards of these values:

$$4 \quad 2 \quad 8 \quad 5 \quad 7$$

"These are my prediction cards, George. If all goes well, some of these will match cards which you will choose completely by chance."

Once more, fan through the deck. This time, remove cards that will match the entire key number. As you remove them, lay them out in their proper order, muttering, "We'll need a variety of cards. These ought to do" (Illus. 96).

George should be side-by-side with you.

"Here we have six cards, George. I'd like you to choose a number to multiply these by. We'll have to select a number completely by chance. So I'd like you to mentally throw a die. If you throw a one, please mentally toss it again, because one

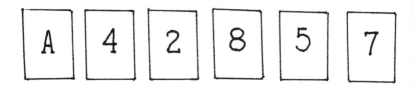

ILLUS. 96

simply duplicates the values we have here. We'll need a two, three, four, five, or six. Now mentally throw that die."

George does so.

"What number did you get?"

He tells you. Suppose he says five. Fan through the deck and remove a 5, placing it below the other cards, as shown in Illus. 97.

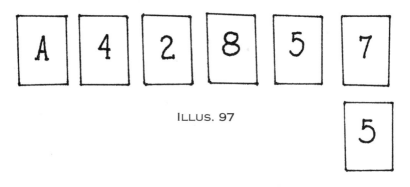

ILLUS. 97

"Now let's do the multiplication together."

You proceed to multiply the number by five. "Five times 7 is 35," you say. "Put down the 5, and carry the 3." Fan through the deck and find a 5; place it below the other cards (Illus. 98).

"Five times 5 is 25," you continue. "Add the 3 that we carried, and we have 28. So we put down the 8, and carry the 2."

Look through the deck and find an 8. Place it to the left of the 5 that you placed down (Illus. 99).

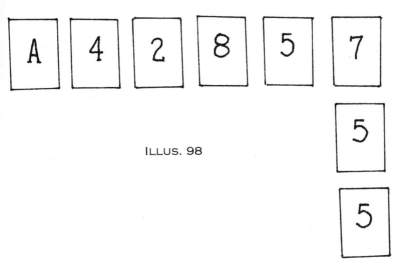

ILLUS. 98

Continue until you complete the entire multiplication process (Illus. 100). In this instance you end up with 714285.

"Is my multiplication correct, George?" It is.

Gather up all the cards that were used in the calculation except for the answer. Turn these face down and place them on top of the deck.

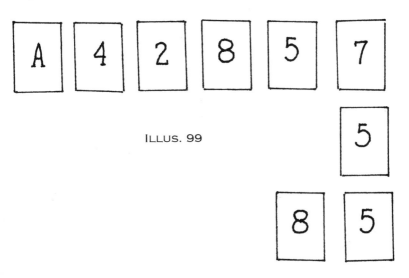

ILLUS. 99

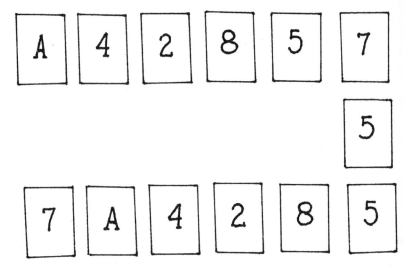

Casually shuffle the cards as you say, "George, please gather up the cards that we arrived at through multiplying by your number. Hold them as you might hold a bridge hand. Sometimes I'm very lucky at bridge. Let's see if that works out here. How many cards do you have?"

He has six cards.

"Oh, you should have five. Let's see . . . we'll eliminate the highest card. I can't remember, what is your highest card . . . a 9?" Eventually, you'll discover that it's an ace. Have him hand it to you. Place it on top of the deck and set the deck aside.

Pick up your prediction pile and hold it the same way that you would hold a bridge hand.

"We each have a five-card hand, George. We'll find out if I'm lucky or not. You arrived at your cards by multiplying some cards by a freely selected number. Let's see if my prediction matches any of your cards. Place one of your cards face up on the table."

He does. "Oh, good! I have one of those." Place the matching card face up on top of his card.

"Let's try another."

He places another one of his cards either face up in another spot on the table, or on top of the other two cards. Either way, you match it.

Continue through the other three cards.

Note

You eliminate the ace from the final revelation because it's the most obvious card in the deck and could possibly tip off the method.

SLICK STICKER TRICK

Master magician Ron Bauer showed me the original trick, which is extremely strong. The only problem is that a bit of preparation is involved and that the performer must be sitting down with a spectator sitting opposite him.

I have come up with four variations which have fewer restrictions. However, you will need a pen. Also, all versions of the trick require the use of those little reminder stickers, ones that are one and a half by two inches in size. A portion of one side has a sticky substance on it for temporarily attaching the paper to something. The product is available at most stores that carry office supplies.

THE ORIGINAL TRICK

Here is the trick that Ron showed me:

You're sitting at a table quite close, with your legs well under the table. Unknown to the group, you have a playing card face down on your lap. On the back of the card is a sticker. Let's say, for example, that the card in your lap with the blank sticker is the 6 of spades.

A group may be gathered around you, but sitting opposite you is Hedda, the person for whom you're performing the trick. Have her shuffle the deck.

Take the deck back and explain, "Hedda, in a moment I'm going to ask you to choose a card. But I'm going to ask you to do it *under the table*, so that the choice will be completely by chance. So I'll hand you the deck face up under the table, and I'd like you to cut off a portion and turn it over, like this."

Demonstrate by holding the deck face up in your left hand. Cut off some cards with your right hand and turn them face down on top of the others. Make sure that Hedda understands. Restore the cards to their original order.

You're now holding the deck face up in your left hand. Take a sticker and affix it to the bottom card, precisely the way the sticker is affixed to the 6 of spades on your lap.

"Hedda, I'm going to write a prediction on the sticker, but I don't want you to see it just yet."

Tilt the cards up so that Hedda cannot see the bottom card. With your pen print this on the sticker: 6S (shorthand for 6 of spades), as shown in Illus. 101.

It doesn't really matter if others see what you print on the sticker.

"Now I'll hand you the cards under the table. And while the cards are still under the table, I want you to cut off a portion and turn it over, just as I showed you."

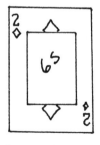

As you near the end of your little speech, place the deck face up under the table with both hands. With your right hand, pick up the face-down 6 of spades and place it, as is, at the face of the deck. Immediately, reach your right hand forward, apparently searching for Hedda's hand.

"Now where's your hand? Ah, here we go."

The situation: You're holding the deck face up in your left hand. On top of the face-up deck is one face-down card, the 6 of spades. On the back of the 6 of spades is a blank sticker. Just below the 6 of spades is the first of the face-up cards. On its face is a sticker with "6S" printed on it.

With your right hand, you've located Hedda's hand. With your left hand, give the deck to Hedda. Bring both hands out from under the table.

In all likelihood, Hedda will feel the sticker on the uppermost card. By no means, mention this!

Just tell her, "When you're done cutting and turning the packet over on top, just bring the cards out."

When she's done, take the cards from her and spread them out onto the table. The uppermost cards will be face down.

Spread out the face-down cards to the point where the face-up cards begin. The first of these will be the 6 of spades that you added under the table (Illus. 102).

The card facing it has the prediction sticker on its face. Point to the 6 of spades, saying, "Here's the card you cut to—the 6 of spades. Now let's take a look at my prediction." Turn

ILLUS. 102

over the card facing it—the last of the face-down cards—revealing your prediction: 6S!

The trick is over. But, if you're going to do more tricks, you must get rid of the sticker on the back of the 6 of spades. The best bet, I believe, is to have a duplicate deck of cards in a card case in your pocket. Take the sticker off your prediction card; then gather up all of the cards, put them into their card case, and place the case into your pocket. If the group wants more magic, remove the duplicate deck from your pocket and proceed.

VARIATIONS

I have four more versions of the trick. All are effective, but each has its strengths and its weaknesses. In all of them, the person for whom you're performing (Hedda) must be seated at a table, but you need not be.

Version 1: This is my favorite.

Again, there is a bit of preparation. Place a sticker on the back of a card. Put this card on the bottom of the deck.

Take out the deck and fan through the cards face down, not quite to the bottom. As you do this, say, "In a moment, I'm going to ask you to select one of these cards, Hedda." (You *don't* want to say anything like, "An ordinary deck of cards," or, "Notice that I haven't put a sticker on the back of any cards.")

Turn the deck face up and fan through several cards from the face of the deck. Note the second card from the bottom; this is your prediction card. Again, let's assume that it's the 6 of spades.

As you fan through the cards, say, "You'll choose any card you wish." Even the cards up and continue. "But first, I'm going to make a prediction. Then I want you to take the deck, cut off a portion, and turn it over like this." Pick up about half and turn the packet over, but don't set it completely down. "Okay?" Return the deck to its original face-up position. The card at the face has a blank sticker on the back. The card below it is the 6 of spades.

As before, place a sticker on the face of the bottom card and print your prediction, 6S. With both hands, take the deck under the table. Turn the uppermost card over.

The situation: The card at the face of the deck now has the blank sticker uppermost; below this card is the 6 of spades. In exactly the same manner as before, give Hedda the deck.

She cuts the cards as directed and brings the deck out. Have her set it on the table.

A bit of "time misdirection" is vital here. So you say something like this: "I had no way of knowing where you'd cut the cards. Yet I had the gall to make a prediction. And if that prediction should work out, it'll prove that I have the ability to foresee the future. Or not."

Spread the cards out onto the table. The top group, of course, consists of face-down cards. The first face-up card has a prediction on its face: 6S. Point this out. Then turn over the last face-down card, showing that it's the 6 of spades.

As in the first version, you must get rid of the extra sticker if you plan to do more tricks.

The reason for the "time misdirection" is that the relative positions of the "sticker" card and the predicted card are illogical; actually, the two should be exchanged. So far, no one has noticed.

Version 2: This one requires no preparation, and you end up with nothing to get rid of.

Have Hedda shuffle the deck. You fan through the cards, both face down and face up, saying, "Hedda, you'll be able to choose any one of these cards that you wish." As you fan through the face-up cards, note the third card from the bottom; this is the card you'll predict. Again, let's assume it's the 6 of spades.

Go through the explanation of how a pile is to be cut off and turned over onto the other cards.

Hold the cards face up, saying, "I'll make a prediction now." Call attention to the bottom card. Let's suppose it's the 5 of diamonds. Turn it over so that it's face down on top of the face-up cards. Put a sticker on it. Tilt the cards up so that Hedda can't see what you print. As always, print 6S on the sticker. This time, you turn the card over again, so that the sticker doesn't show. Explain to Hedda, "I don't want you to see the prediction yet."

Hand the cards to Hedda beneath the table in the usual manner. This time, however, you turn over the two uppermost cards together before handing the deck over.

The situation: Uppermost is a face-down card (of no significance). Below it is the face-down 5 of diamonds, with a sticker on the back; the sticker is marked 6S. Below this card is the first face-up card, the 6 of spades.

Hedda performs the cut as directed and brings the deck forth. Again, she sets it onto the table. Since the two critical cards will not be in their logical positions, you again use some "time misdirection."

Then you spread the cards out onto the table. You turn over the last face-down card, showing that it's the 6 of spades. Call attention to the first face-up card, the 5 of diamonds. Turn it over and show your prediction.

You're all set to perform more tricks. But you've lost the feature in which the spectator can feel the sticker on the card.

Version 3: Here, the second card from the bottom has a blank sticker on its back.

You start by fanning through the face-down cards, almost to the bottom. And then fan through the face-up cards, noting the third card from the bottom—as usual, the 6 of spades.

You explain how to cut the cards.

A sticker is placed on the face of the bottom card. You tilt the deck toward yourself and print 6S on the sticker.

As in the previous version, you turn over the uppermost two cards together before handing Hedda the deck. When Hedda brings the deck out, you again use "time misdirection."

When you spread the deck out, you fan through to the first face-up card, which shows your prediction. And you show the last face-down card, which is the card you predicted (the 6 of spades).

The advantage is that the spectator feels the sticker; the disadvantage is that you must get rid of the extra sticker.

Version 4: In some respects, this is the best version of the bunch: There is no setup, the position of the critical cards is logical, and there's no cleanup. But you lose the advantage of the spectator feeling the sticker.

The deck is shuffled by Hedda. You take the deck back, saying, "Hedda, you'll have complete freedom in choosing any one of these cards." You hold the deck face down and rapidly fan through about a quarter of the deck. Close up the deck and turn it face up. Fan through about a quarter of the deck again. As you do so, note and remember the bottom card. Let's say it's the 6 of spades.

Turn the deck *face down*. Demonstrate how Hedda is supposed to take the face-down cards, cut off a portion, turn it over, and place it on top of the other cards.

Turn the top card face up and put a sticker on it. In the usual way, make your prediction—print 6S. Turn the card face down.

Before handing Hedda the deck under the table, slip the bottom card to the top, turning it face up in the process.

When Hedda brings the deck out, the top portion is face up and the bottom portion face down. You spread the cards out onto the table. The last face-up card contains your prediction on its face—just as it should. And the first face-down card is the 6 of spades, your prediction card.

Note

I understand that this trick is derived from one in which stickers were not used—the prediction was made on a card with a marking pen. This can be very effective, if you don't mind losing a card now and then. See how this method might work out with some of my variations, particularly with the last variation, Version 4.

COINCIDENCE OR UNEXPLAINABLE CONCURRENCE

LUCKY IN LOVE

This trick is calculated to make everyone feel good, particularly the person who volunteers to assist you.

A bit of preparation is necessary. Take any nine black cards from the deck and place them on top. On top of these, put the queen of hearts.

Jim is a bachelor with no particular attachment to a young lady, so he would be the perfect choice to assist you.

Once you have enlisted Jim's help, casually fan off ten cards from the top of the deck and hand them to him, saying, "We'll just need a small packet of cards."

You should keep the cards in the same order. This can be easily done by counting the cards in groups of three as you fan them out, taking them—one under the other—into the right hand.

"Jim, we want to find out whether you'll be lucky in love. So I'd like you to think of a number that you really like—some number from, say, one to ten. It could be a lucky number, a number that has some significance in your life, or—if all else fails—a number that simply occurs to you."

Continue, "Do you have your number? Good. Now I'll turn my back and I'd like you to transfer that many cards, one at a time, from the top to the bottom of your packet. For instance, if your number were 3, you'd move three cards one at a time to the bottom of your packet."

Turn away. When you turn back, take the packet from Jim, saying, "We'd better mix these a bit." Transfer ten cards from the top to the bottom of the packet, using the "One–Two–Three Shift," described starting on page 22. This, of course, keeps the packet in the same order.

Deal the top card face down onto the table to the right. On top of it, and overlapping to the right, deal the next card. The third

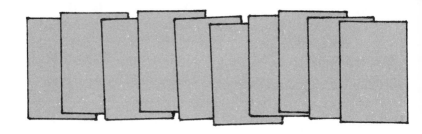

ILLUS. 103

card also overlaps to the right. Continue until the entire packet is dealt out. (Illus. 103 is from your point of view.) Perform this deal fairly rapidly and, as you do so, say, "So here's your packet."

A bit of "time misdirection" would be appropriate here.

"Obviously, Jim, I have no way of knowing what number you chose. As we all know, it could be any number from one to ten. So now I'd like you to use that number to select a card. Just count to that number in this packet." As you utter the last sentence, start at your right side of the spread, touching first the top card of the bunch, then the second card, and finally the third card. This shows him precisely how he is to count.

If Jim counts to his card aloud, fine. But if he counts silently, mentally count along with him. Suppose he stops with his finger resting on the seventh card. You make sure he got it right by saying, "So you thought of the number seven, right?"

Have him slide his selection away from the other cards. "But don't look at your card just yet. Let's see what you might have picked."

Turn over all the other cards. All of them are black. "You could have chosen one of these very negative cards. So let's see what you picked."

He turns over the queen of hearts.

"The queen of hearts! The symbol of love. Jim, you're really going to be lucky in love."

Notes

1) The trick may done in exactly the same way for a woman.

2) If your assistant is in a happy relationship with a person of the opposite sex, you simply change the wording at the beginning: "We want to find out if you are lucky in love."

THREE-CARD COINCIDENCE

I believe Martin Gardner invented this trick and that Nick Trost developed what I consider a stronger version. I have added a slight twist to the Trost trick.

GROUP 1

Remove from the deck the ace, 2, and 3 of clubs, hearts, and diamonds. As you take them from the deck, toss them face up onto the table. Set the rest of the deck aside.

Nora believes in ESP, for all you know, so ask her to assist you.

GROUP 2

"If we both concentrate, Nora, this experiment is sure to work. In fact, if we both have the proper attitude this should be as easy as one, two, three. That's why I have three sets of 'one-two-three' right here on the table."

GROUP 3

Go through the cards on the table and form three face-up groups, each consisting of an ace, a two, and a three. Each set of three should include a club, a heart, and a diamond. *Make sure the cards are spread out so that you can tell the order of the suits.* Let's say that the three groups are those shown in Illus. 104.

Address Nora, "Please select one of the groups of three for yourself. Just pick up one of the groups."

Let's say she picks up Group 1.

"Good. Now which group should we leave on the table face up?"

We'll assume that she selects Group 2. Pick up Group 2. Before proceeding, look at the remaining group and note the order of the suits from the bottom up. In this instance, you note that the order of suits in Group 3 is clubs, diamonds, hearts. Deal Group 2 into a face-up row so that, from left to right, the suits are in the same order as Group 3 (Illus. 105).

Pick up Group 3 and hold it face down.

The situation: We have three groups of cards consisting of ace, two, and three of different suits. Nora is holding Group 1. Face up in a row on the table is Group 2. You're holding Group 3. Your top card matches the suit of Group 2's card on the left. Your second card matches the suit of Group 2's middle card. And your bottom card matches the suit of Group 2's card on the right.

"Apparently, I get this group, Nora. I'll put them down here."

ILLUS. 105

Deal your three cards in a face-down row aligned just below Group 2 (Illus. 106).

"It's your turn, Nora. Without letting me see any cards, I'd like you to put your cards face down in a row right here." Indicate a spot above Group 2. "When you put your cards down, make sure you don't match any of the face-up cards in value. In other words, don't put a two below a two."

When she finishes, say, "I already know you did a perfect job." Turn each of the Group 2 cards face down in place, saying, "We'll forget these."

Point to her cards. "Put your hand on one of your cards. I'll touch my matching card—the card in the same column. We'll turn them over together and see how we match up."

There are now two possible endings:

Ending 1: Nora and you turn over two corresponding cards. They are of the same value.

"They match!" you shriek. Place your card face up on top of her face-up card. Again you turn over two corresponding cards, and again they match in value. And, of course, the remaining two also match in value.

Ending 2: Nora and you turn over two corresponding cards. They are of the same *suit.* You are far more excited about this than she is.

"Look at that!" you declare, utterly astounded. "They're both the same suit." Place your card face up on top of her face-up card. You go through the procedure twice more, matching the suit each time.

"I wonder if it's possible that . . . Let's see." Turn over Group 3's card on the left. It's the same suit as the others in its column. Place it face up on top of the other two cards. "Ah, a perfect group of three!"

Repeat with the middle card of Group 3 and then the card on the right. All three cards in each column are of the same suit.

With either ending, you have quite a coincidence.

Lucky Numbers

This is my version of a Peter Wilker trick in which he used an old principle to fashion an astonishing mental trick. Beforehand, take the two red queens from the deck. Place one on top of the deck and one on the bottom.

Jenny enjoys a good card trick, so she'll probably be happy to help you out. Set the deck onto the table and say, "Jenny, would you please cut off about half the cards and place them onto the table next to the others."

After she does this, pick up the original lower portion of the deck, saying, "Let's see how close you came to half." Count the cards aloud as you take them one on top of the other. (If you prefer, you can count them into a pile on the table.) Whatever number you end up with, say, "That's amazing. You just gave them a casual cut, and you came extremely close to cutting them exactly in half. Now I know this experiment is going to work."

At this point a red queen is on top of each pile.

Place the piles side by side. "In magic, Jenny, there are two really significant numbers—seven and 13. We're going to use both of them in this experiment. Let's start with seven. Please give me any number from one to seven."

Suppose she chooses four. Counting aloud, you deal four cards simultaneously from each pile, placing each card face down next to its pile. In other words, you deal to the right of the pile on the right, and to the left of the pile on the left.

Turn over the top card of each of the piles you dealt off. Usually, the cards will be quite different in suit and value. Comment on their differences.

If their suits or colors happen to be the same, mention, "Good! That's a start."

If the cards happen to be of the same value, say, "This is amazing. Four must be your lucky number."

Turn the two cards face down and replace them on the dealt-off piles. Place the dealt-off piles back onto their original piles. "Now, Jenny, let's try the number 13. Please give me any number higher than seven but not more than 13."

Let's say she chooses 11. As before, deal off that number to the side of each pile. Again show the top card of each pile you dealt off. Comment on the cards, calling attention to their similarities and differences. Replace these cards face down on top of their respective counted-off piles. Place the counted-off piles back onto their original piles.

"So far," you say, "we haven't accomplished much. But let's see if your two chosen numbers have *combined* power. Your numbers were four and 11. So we'll start with four."

As before, you simultaneously deal the cards to the side of each packet. With the first card, you say, "Four." With the next, you say, "Five." Continue until you deal the card numbered 11.

"Jenny, let's see if these cards in any way match." Turn them over and hold them side by side. "Perfect! How symbolic! You chose two beautiful ladies."

Notes

1) If you do the trick for a man, you might prefer to use kings or jacks. At the end, you comment, "You chose two handsome men."

2) When dealing the cards simultaneously, you might find it easier to pick the cards off from the rear, fingers on top, and thumb below.

WHAT A COINCIDENCE!

I believe it was the legendary mentalist Ted Annemann who came up with this psychological force.

The problem is this: Occasionally, the force doesn't work. What do you do? You might indicate that since mentalism isn't an exact science, you can't always be perfect. Or you might explain that the vibrations weren't just right. Still, it would be nice to have some sort of satisfactory solution when you miss. I have a method here that works quite well.

The critical cards are these: king of hearts, 7 of clubs, ace of diamonds, 4 of hearts, and the 9 of diamonds. They are laid out in a row so that the spectator sees them in this order, the king of hearts being on his left.

You can remove these five cards from the deck one at a time and then lay them out in the proper order. Or you may prefer to have them sitting on top of the deck, ready for you to casually deal them into a face-up row.

The cards are laid out. Say to Bernie, "I wonder if you'd help me out. We have five cards here, and I'd like you to think of one.

"But before you do, I want you to look them over carefully so that your choice will be completely free. For instance, you might choose the king of hearts. Or maybe you think a face card is too obvious.

"Or you could choose the 7 of clubs—a lucky card. But then it's the only black card.

"You could take the ace of diamonds, but maybe an ace is also too obvious. I don't know.

"The 4 of hearts? Some people associate hearts with romance, but others are reminded of a serious operation. It all depends.

"The 9 of diamonds? Diamonds are forever. Maybe that's a good choice; maybe not.

"I'll look away while you think of one."

After he has one, turn back and pick up the five cards. Give them a little overhand shuffle. "Please concentrate on your card, Bernie."

Fan through the cards, faces towards yourself, as though studying them. From time to time, remove a card. Shake your head and replace it in the fan.

Continue moving cards around. Actually, you're setting them up so that from top to bottom (if the packet were face down) the order is 4, 7, 9, king, ace—in other words, from lowest to highest.

"Bernie, we have to establish contact between you, the cards, and me." Set the packet of five onto the table. "Please give the cards a cut." He does so. Perhaps have him do it again.

"Good!" Pick up the packet, glance at the faces, and cut the cards so that the 7 becomes the bottom card (the card at the face of the packet). The order of the cards is now 9, king, ace, 4, 7. You're holding the cards in a fan, faces toward yourself.

"Bernie, you're thinking of your card, right? Now I'll give you a card which will indicate your thought."

Remove the 4 of hearts and place it face down onto his extended palm. "Please place your other hand on top of it. Good. Now you're holding the card and there's no way in the world I can change it." Pause. "Name your card."

He names the 4 of hearts. "Please show everyone the card you're holding."

That's what happens most of the time. But Bernie might choose another card, just to annoy you.

You have alternatives. These are not necessarily wonderful, but they do provide an adequate conclusion in the rare instances when the 4 is not chosen.

The packet is set up so that you can spell out any of the other four cards. The remaining possibilities are 7, 9, king, ace—again, lowest to highest. You'll spell F–O–U–R for the seven and nine; you'll spell F–O–U–R and then H–E–A–R–T–S for the king and ace.

So, if Bernie names the 7 or 9, you say, "Turn over the card, please." He does. "As I said, the 4 should indicate your thought."

If Bernie names the king or ace, tell him to turn over the card.

Continue: "As I said, the 4 of hearts should indicate your thought." In either instance, add: "Let's see if it works."

Let's say Bernie has said that his card is the 7 of clubs.

"We'll spell out 'four.' "

Say the letter F, moving one card from the top to the bottom of the packet. Do the same for the letters O and U. When you say the letter R, however, turn over the top card. It's the 7.

If Bernie says that his card is the 9 (next highest), spell out F–O–U–R, moving one card from top to bottom for each letter. Turn up the card now on top. It's the 9.

The next highest card is the king. You have told Bernie that the 4 of hearts should indicate his thought. Continue: "First, we have the 'four.' "

Spell out F–O–U–R, moving one card from top to bottom for each letter.

"Then 'hearts.' "

Spell H–E–A–R–T–S, moving one card from top to bottom for each letter except the S. When you say the letter S, turn over the top card, showing the king.

For the ace, spell out F–O–U–R, exactly as you did for the king. Then spell H–E–A–R–T–S, moving one card from top to bottom for each letter. Turn over the card that is now on top. It's the ace.

THE FIRST QUADRUPLE COINCIDENCE

A few years ago I invented a trick that I called "Quadruple Coincidence." Soon after, I came across an older trick of the same name, invented, I believe, by Frank Garcia. Offhand, I can't think of a better impromptu trick. It dawned on me a short while ago that a basic component of the trick is a discovery of mine from many, many years ago.

Phil doesn't believe in mentalism in any form, so he's the perfect assistant. Hand him the deck of cards and ask him to shuffle.

Take the deck back and hold it up so that the back of the deck is toward the spectators.

"I need a prediction card," you declare. Note the value of the bottom card.

Hold the deck face up so that all can see the cards. With your right hand, take the bottom card. Take the next card *on top of this*. Continue dealing cards, one on top of the other, until you've taken as many cards as you need to *spell out* the value of the bottom card.

For instance, suppose the bottom card is a 3. As you take the cards, one on top of the other, into your right hand, spell to yourself, "T–H–R–E–E," taking one card for each letter. Place these five cards face down on the table to your right. So, on the table is a pile of five cards, the top card of which is the one you saw on the bottom of the deck, a 3.

"Don't worry, I'll find a good prediction card." Again, start taking cards one on top of the other into your right hand until you come to a card which matches the original bottom card— in this instance, another 3. The 3, then, is the last card you take into your right hand. Turn the cards in your right hand face down and place the group on top of the pile on the table. In our example, you now have two threes together, fifth and sixth from the bottom of the face-down pile on the table.

"Need a prediction," you mumble. At this point, if you wish, you can stop taking the cards one on top of the other; instead, just fan rapidly through the cards until you come to another 3. This 3 you cut to the *back* of the face-up cards you're holding. (In other words, the 3 would be the top card if the packet were face down.)

At this point, tilt the deck toward you so that spectators can't see the faces of the cards. Fan through to the fourth 3. Without letting the group see its face, place this 3 face down well in front of you.

"At last, my prediction!"

Place the rest of the cards in your hand face down onto the pile on the table. In our example, a face-down 3 is set forward as your prediction card, the top card of the deck is a 3, and the fifth and sixth cards from the bottom are threes.

Pick up the deck and turn it face up. Rapidly deal the cards into a face-up pile. After you've dealt 15 or so, say to Phil, "You can tell me to stop anytime."

When you're told to stop, pick up the pile you've dealt off, turn it face down, and set it down to your right. Place the packet remaining in your left hand face down to your left.

"You chose when to stop, Phil. Now please touch one of the piles. We'll use the one you choose."

Suppose he chooses the pile on your left. "All right," you say. Turn over the top card of the pile and replace it, face up, onto the pile. "So you chose a 3. Let's spell that out." Pick up the other pile. Spell T–H–R–E–E aloud, dealing one card into a pile for each letter in the spelling.

If Phil should touch the pile on your right, say, "All right, we'll spell down in the pile you've chosen." As before, you turn

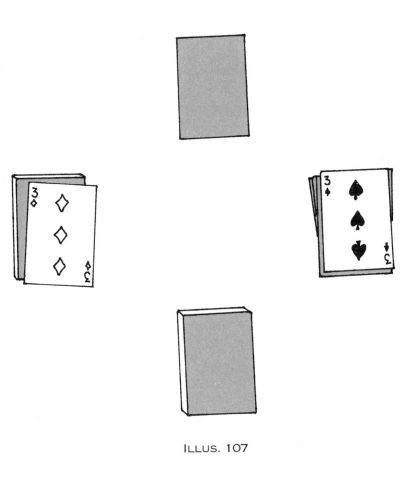

over the top card of the pile on the left and spell out that value in the pile on your right.

In either instance, you touch the last card dealt out and say, "Wouldn't it be a coincidence if this turned out to be a 3 also?" Turn the card over, showing that it is a 3, and place it face up on top of the others you dealt off. Place the remainder of the deck directly in front of you.

The cards on the table should now form a diamond pattern, as in Illus. 107.

"Wouldn't it be even more of a coincidence if my prediction card turned out to be a similar card?"

Turn over your prediction, showing it to be a 3.

Touch the pile directly in front of you. "And what must this card be?" Turn it over to show that it also is a 3.

Review

1) A spectator shuffles the deck. You take it back, saying, "I need a prediction card."

2) Hold the deck face up and note the value of the bottom card. Let's assume that it's a 3. Silently spell out the value of this card, taking one card under the other for each letter. In this instance, spell out T–H–R–E–E. Place this pile face down onto the table.

3) Continue going through the deck, taking one card on top of the other, until you come to another 3, which will be the last card you take into your right hand. Place this pile face down on top of the first pile.

4) Fan rapidly through the cards until you come to a third 3. Cut the cards so that this three becomes the top card.

5) Tilt the deck toward you so that others can't see the cards. Fan through to the fourth 3. Without letting anyone else see its face, place it face down well forward of you. "At last, my prediction!"

6) Place the rest of the cards in your hand face down on top of the pile on the table. Pick up the deck and turn it face up. Rapidly deal the cards into a face-up pile. After dealing 15 or so, ask a spectator to tell you when to stop.

7) When stopped, turn the dealt-off cards face down. Place the remaining cards in your hand face down to the left of this pile.

8) Ask a spectator to choose one of the piles. If he takes the one on your left, you turn over the top card of that pile and

say, "So you chose a 3. Let's spell that out." Pick up the other pile and spell T–H–R–E–E, dealing out one card for each letter in the spelling.

9) If the spectator chooses the pile on your right, say, "We'll spell down in the pile you've chosen." As before, turn over the top card of the pile on your left and spell out the value in the other pile.

10) Indicate that you're hoping for a coincidence as you turn over the last card you dealt out in the spelling. It is also a 3. Turn it face up and place it on top of the cards you just dealt out.

11) Place the remainder of the deck directly in front of you. The cards should now form a diamond pattern.

12) Turn over your prediction card, showing that it's also a 3.

13) Turn over the top card of the remainder of the deck; it's the fourth three.

Notes

1) Once in a while, this happens at the beginning of the trick: You note the bottom card and start to spell out its value, taking cards into your right hand. But one of these cards is of the same value as the bottom card. Obviously, the trick won't work. Give the deck a quick shuffle and start again.

2) The placing of the four cards in a diamond formation is not only visually pleasing, but also provides a dramatic touch which enhances the trick considerably. It makes sense, therefore, to pause after the revelation of the fourth card, letting all enjoy the configuration and the startling climax.

IS MY FACE RED?

A familiar theme in card magic is this: Spectators try to guess whether face-down cards are red or black, with perfect success. In this version, I have superimposed some humor and excellent spectator participation.

Furthermore, I have developed a way of secretly setting up the deck while spectators watch.

Solicit the aid of Cathie and Dobie. Have them each give the deck a shuffle.

Take the cards back, saying, "Cathie and Dobie, I'd like you to participate in a little contest. We'll see which one of you is better at identifying colors."

Fan the cards out, faces toward you. Pick out a card and hold it up, its back toward Cathie.

"Is this card red, Cathie? Yes or no." Whatever she answers, show the face of the card. Comment on her decision. Set the card aside face down.

Show Dobie the back of a card. Ask him, "Is this card black, Dobie? Yes or no." He answers; you show him the face of the card, make a comment, and set the card aside, on top of Cathie's first choice.

Again show Cathie the back of a card, asking her if it's red. Go through the same procedure as before. Repeat the process with Dobie, asking him if his card is black.

You continue, asking Cathie if she thinks the card is red and then asking Dobie if he thinks his card is black. Sometimes the card you hold up for Cathie is red, and sometimes it's black. And the same for Dobie. Each time that you set a card aside, you add it to a face-down pile.

Just keep going. For how long? For however long it takes you to get your cards set up.

When you first fan out the cards, you'll notice that, near the bottom, a number of red and black cards alternate. If this is not the case, cut the cards so that you do have a concentration of alternating reds and blacks near the bottom. You may find such a group with a few odd cards breaking up the perfect sequence. You will pick out these cards for Cathie and Dobie to guess.

Let's suppose that after Cathie and Dobie have made a few guesses, you have eight cards on the bottom alternating in color. Lift these off and place them onto the table in a face-down pile.

Give the remainder of the deck a little overhand shuffle. Turn the deck faces toward you again. Continue playing the game with Cathie and Dobie while actually you set up another bottom section to alternate reds and blacks. Again, if there is a preponderance of one color, you might have to cut the cards or even give them another shuffle. And feel free to shift a card or two as you try to decide which card to hold up next.

After Cathie and Dobie make additional guesses, you might have six, eight, or ten cards in appropriate alternating order. Place these face down on top of the pile you already have on the table.

You continue the process until you have at least 20 cards in the pile on the table.

Two things you must attend to:

1) Always place an even number of cards onto the table.
2) Remember the color of the original bottom card.

Following these two rules, you'll never get confused; you'll always end up with an even number of cards, and the cards will always alternate perfectly.

Let's suppose that the bottom card of the first pile is black. You must make sure that any other pile you place on top of it also has a black card on the bottom. And, since all piles are of an even number, the eventual top card will always be red.

This guessing procedure with Cathie and Dobie doesn't actually take very long. After each has made no more than five or six guesses, you should have your pile set up.

Meanwhile, you've been commenting on the choices made. Perhaps one contestant has been doing better than the other. In all probability, both have missed at least a few.

"That was the warm-up," you say. "Now we'll play for real. But I want each of you to do as well as you possibly can, so I'm going to place you both under a hypnotic spell." Wave your hands hypnotically before Cathie and Dobie. "You are weary, very weary. You are tired . . . tired. Bored, even. Now you're both under my spell. Will the miracles never stop?"

While gabbing away, set the balance of the deck on top of the pile of cards that Cathie and Dobie have guessed. Even up your pile of alternating reds and blacks. "Now you each must give this pile a cut." Make sure each gives the pile one *complete* cut. After they finish, pick up the cards and briefly tap them on the table on their long sides to even them up. The faces of the cards are toward you.

Actually, you're taking a peek at the bottom card to see what color it is.

If the bottom card is black, then the top card must be red; and vice versa. So let's say that when you peek at the bottom card, you see that it's black. Since Cathie has always been asked if she thinks the card is *red*, she must begin.

Set the packet between the two contestants.

Say to Cathie, "Do you think the top card is red, Cathie?"

If she says yes, continue, "Then just take that top card and, without looking at it, put it face down in front of you."

If she says no, say, "Then just take that top card and, without looking at it, place it on top of the rest of the deck." Indicate the pile where you put the previously guessed cards and the balance of the deck.

Ask Dobie if he thinks the next top card is black. If he thinks so, he places the card face down in front of him. Otherwise, he places it on top of the remainder of the deck.

"Your turn, Cathie. Is it red?" She makes her decision, and Dobie then decides if the next card is black.

They continue until the pile is exhausted. You, of course, interject comments, like, "Well, you have to take *some* cards," or, "They can't *all* be black."

Pick up the discards and casually give them a little shuffle as you proceed. "Let's see who the winner is. Turn your cards over, Cathie." She does. When she spreads them out, everyone sees that they're all red.

"And now you, Dobie." He has all black cards.

"A tie!" you declare. "You both got them all right."

Pause.

"I'd like to congratulate you, but my hypnotic spell did the job. I'm going to keep you under that spell so that you'll both be absolutely *right*—for the rest of your lives."

A Psychic Test

In its effect, this trick is somewhat similar to the preceding one. The basic secret is well known among magicians. I have made several changes in both presentation and method to eliminate sleight of hand and to make the trick impromptu.

Start by asking Lorne if he has any psychic powers. Whatever he replies, say, "I know that you have strong psychic powers, Lorne. In fact, I feel that you're sending me a mental message that you'd like me to test those powers of yours. Would you like to do that?"

He accepts the invitation.

You take a deck of cards, saying, "We'll need 13 pairs for this test," you say, "each pair a red and a black. I know that 13 is bad luck, but I think it might turn out to be a good-luck number for you."

Fan through the cards face up so that all can see. Remove from the deck a pair of cards—one black, one red. The black card should be uppermost. As you remove the pair, say to yourself, "Black and red." Make sure everyone sees the pair (Illus. 108).

Turn the pair face down and set it on the table, saying, "One pair." Pause. "Would you all keep count with me. We must have exactly 13 pairs."

Take out another mixed pair, this time with the red card uppermost. As you do so, say to yourself, "Red and black."

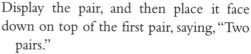

Display the pair, and then place it face down on top of the first pair, saying, "Two pairs."

Continue alternating black-and-red pairs with red-and-black pairs until you have 13 pairs in a face-down pile. You now have a red card on top, followed by a pair of blacks, a pair of reds, a pair of blacks, and so forth. The bottom card is black, and you have a pair of reds above it.

Set aside the rest of the deck. Even up the pile and have the packet cut three times, because "three is a lucky number." After three cuts, the deck is still set up in a continuous series of pairs, which match in color. (There could be a single black card or a single red card on the bottom; if so, it will match in color the card on top.) Two cards, however, break up this series; they are the original top and bottom cards of the packet. Thumb through the packet, faces toward yourself, until you find these two cards (Illus. 109).

In Illus. 109, on the following page, you can see that the 2 of spades and the ace of hearts are the two that break up the series. Once they are removed, the series of red and black pairs will be perfect.

Here's how you remove them: Say, "We'll need a couple of markers." With the cards still facing you, cut the deck so that these two cards come to the top. In this instance, you cut the cards so that the two of spades comes to the top, while the second card from the top is the ace of hearts. Turn the packet face down.

Deal the top card face up onto the table, saying, "A black card." Deal the present top card face up onto the table next to the first card, saying, "And a red card." Turn the packet face down and set it on the table. You now have a pair of black cards on top, followed by alternating pairs of red and black.

"Lorne, we have 12 pairs left. If you get six of these right, that would be about average. But I *know* that you have psychic powers, so my guess is that you'll get at least seven or eight of these right."

Lift off the top two cards from the packet on the table. Mix them a bit as you say, "Which one of these cards do you think is black?"

Since both cards are black, his chances of getting it right are excellent. Whichever he chooses, place it face down on the black marker. Place the other card on top of the remainder of the deck.

Treat the next pair the same way, asking him to choose which card he thinks is red. Continue through the rest of the pairs, alternating the colors. At the end, you show that he did not get seven or eight right—he got them *all* right.

"Good heavens, Lorne! You're far more psychic than I thought you were."

ILLUS. 109

**THE 2 OF SPADES AND THE ACE
OF HEARTS BREAK UP THE PATTERN.**

Note

If you start by asking the spectator which card he thinks is the red one, and continue alternating colors, he will miss every one. This can be amusing, proving that he has no psychic ability whatever (or has *inverse* psychic ability). But I prefer the other version, which is more upbeat and leaves everyone happy.

They Always Get Their Man

This is my slight variation of a trick by Phil Goldstein. I changed the working a bit and the patter quite a bit.

Fan through the deck and toss the red jacks face up onto the table.

Explain to the group, "You've probably heard stories of the valiant Canadian Mounted Police, or, as they are sometimes known, the Mounties. Who can tell me what they're best known for?"

Someone is bound to get the right answer: "They always get their man."

"That's right. And we're going to put that theory to the test. We'll see if the sterling qualities of the Mounties can be transferred to the playing cards which represent them."

Point to the face-up red jacks on the table.

"Here we have two Mounties. I'm sure you notice their traditional red jackets."

Rosemarie has always had an interest in officers of the law, so ask her to assist you.

Casually fan seven cards from the top of the deck. Lift them off and hand them to Rosemarie, saying, "Rosemarie, I'd like you to pick a criminal from those cards. You can either choose one from the underworld . . ." Indicate the bottom card of the packet: ". . . or you can choose one from the top echelons of crime."

Indicate the top card.

"So, when you're done shuffling, look at either the top or bottom card. But don't do it just yet. After you've chosen a criminal, you'll perform a peculiar shuffle. Then I'll put one of the Mounties on top of the packet and one on the bottom, and you'll perform the same kind of shuffle again. But you don't have to remember all of that. We'll take it step by step. So, when you're ready, look at the top or bottom card."

If she looks at the *top* card, she performs an *under-down* shuffle: She places the top card on the bottom of the packet, the next card onto the table, the next card on the bottom, the next card on top of the one on the table, etc. When she is left with one card in her hand, she places this on top of those on the table.

You lead her through the shuffle, saying, "Put the top card on the bottom of the packet, deal the next card onto the table, put the next one on the bottom of the packet . . ."

If she looks at the *bottom* card, she performs a *down-under* shuffle. The first card goes onto the table, the next one on the bottom of the packet, the next onto the table, etc. And, as before, the last card she holds goes onto the pile on the table. Again, lead her through the shuffle.

"So now our criminal is buried somewhere in the packet. These two jacks are supposed to be Mounties, so let's see if they can behave like Mounties. The packet you're holding, Rosemarie, represents a big mountain with thousands of trees on it. The Mounties know that the criminal is somewhere on the mountain, so they're going to search it from top to bottom."

Hand her one of the red jacks face up. "Please put one Mountie on top of the packet face up." Hand her the other jack. "And put the other Mountie on the bottom of the packet face up."

When she finishes, hold out your left hand palm up. "Please place the packet onto my hand."

After she does, place your right hand on top and give the cards a quick shake. "This gets them started on their search." Lift up your right hand and have her take the packet back.

"Now, Rosemarie, you must take them on their search."

This time, she will *always* perform an under-down shuffle. "Put the top card on the bottom, deal the next card onto the table, put the next card on the bottom, deal the next card on top of the card on the table."

If necessary, take her through it the rest of the way. In all likelihood, however, she won't need any coaching after the first two cards.

Take the cards from the table. Fan them out. Fan down to the face-up red jacks. Between them is a face-down card. Remove all three together and set them onto the table. *Put the rest of the cards on top of the deck.*

"Well, the Mounties captured someone. Let's see how they did. Rosemarie, what's the name of the criminal you chose?"

After she names the card, you turn over the "captured" card.

"So the Mounties got their man. But how did those jacks *know* they were Mounties?

"And how did they find their man? Who knows? You know what I think? I think it's just coincidence."

At this point, you'll probably get some sarcastic comments from the group.

Notes

1) Putting the remainder of the packet back on top at the end of the trick is important. A spectator trying to reconstruct the trick will find it extremely difficult without knowing the correct number of cards. In fact, after the trick is over, a spectator will sometimes ask, "How many cards did you give me?" As usual, I lie, saying, "I don't know. I didn't notice." This clearly implies that the number is irrelevant.

2) Early on, you tell your assistant that she'll perform a peculiar shuffle and that later, she'll perform the same kind of shuffle. But even when she performs a down-under shuffle the first time, she *must* perform an under-down shuffle the second time. Does this make you an obvious liar? Not really. The

shuffles are the "same kind;" they're just not identical. So far, no one has called me on there being a difference between the two. If anyone ever says to me, "Hey, those two shuffles are different," I'll reply, "Of course," and continue on.

A Subtle Touch

As far as I know, the method involved here is my invention. The main feature of the trick is that you never touch the cards.

Hand Francine the deck and ask her to mix the cards. When she finishes and tries to return the deck to you, comment, "No, no. I want the deck to remain in your hands throughout the experiment."

Pause to make sure this selling point sinks in. "Now I'd like you to deal the cards into a face-up pile. Deal as many as you want. I'll turn my back, so when you're done, be sure to tell me. Otherwise, this could be an extremely long experiment. Go ahead, you can start dealing."

As Francine begins dealing, you count the first several cards mentally to get the pace. Then you turn away, but continue to count at the same pace. When Francine says she's done, stop counting. But be sure to remember the number you counted to—your *key number*.

With your back still turned to the group, give Francine these directions: "Look at the last card you dealt and remember it. That's your chosen card. Now pick up the pile you dealt off, turn it face down, and put it back on top of the deck."

When Francine is done, you turn and face the group once more. Now you have a bit of simple math to do. You subtract 8 from your key number. Let's suppose your key number is 14. You subtract 8, giving you 6.

"Francine, I need to find my lucky card. Please slowly deal the cards into a face-up pile. When you get to my lucky card, I'll stop you."

Actually, you're not looking for a lucky card; you want to

stop her after she has dealt out the sixth card. Why the sixth card? Because 6 is the result of subtracting 8 from your key number, 14.

If you had counted to 19 originally, then 19 would be your key number. You'd subtract 8 from 19, getting 11. In this instance, you'd stop Francine after she had dealt 11 cards.

Back to our original example: Francine has dealt out six cards face up and you've stopped her. But you don't simply stop her; after all, you want to conceal the fact that you've been counting.

So here's what you do: Suppose the sixth card she deals is the 9 of clubs; you say, "That's it! The 9 of clubs—my lucky card!" Naturally, she stops dealing.

"I'm going to need my lucky card, so would you please hand it to me. It's curious, but nearly every time I hold my lucky card, a peculiar coincidence occurs. Let's see if it happens again." She gives you the card. Point to the remaining cards that she just dealt out. "Turn these face down on the table."

She does. "Please put the rest of the deck on top of the pile."

After she's done, say, "For this to work, Francine, you'll have to deal out five cards in a row. So far, you've done all the dealing face up, so you might as well continue doing that."

She does so. Continue, with appropriate pauses: "Now deal another card face up on top of each one. Continue until you have seven face-up cards in each pile. As we all know, seven is one of the most powerful numbers in magic."

After Francine has finished dealing, her chosen card should be second from the bottom (or sixth from the face) in one of the five face-up piles.

"I feel strongly that your card is in one of the piles, Francine."

Hold your lucky card up to your ear and listen intently for a moment.

"In fact, my lucky card is sure of it. Are we right?"

You are. "Good. Please pick up that pile."

Francine is holding the pile face up. "Just a second," you say.

Hold your lucky card up to your ear again and listen for a moment.

"My lucky card says that you should do a down-under shuffle. If all goes well, you'll end up with your chosen card. Just deal that first card onto the table. Then put the next card on the bottom of your pile. The next card goes on the table, and the next one goes to the bottom of the pile."

Francine continues until she's holding one face-up card.

"Don't keep us in suspense, Francine. Is that your card?"

It is.

The only time the trick fails is when Francine changes her pace when originally dealing out the cards. Even then, the trick might work, because you can be off as many as two cards on either side of the correct number and still be successful.

So, unlikely as the possibility is, suppose the trick just didn't work. What do you do? I don't know. The one time that it happened to me, I blamed my lucky card and declared vehemently that I was dumping it and getting myself a new lucky card.

TELEPATHY, OR THOUGHT TRANSFERENCE

THE ACTING MAGICIAN

Are you a good actor? If not, here you have a chance to sharpen up your acting skills.

If you *are* a good actor, this trick is perfect for you. I developed this trick to take advantage of my own ability to appear utterly serious as I present the most inane propositions. The principle used here is quite venerable.

At the beginning, you must know the names of the top and bottom cards. Rather than strain my memory, I usually place the ace of spades on top of the deck and the ace of clubs on the bottom. Let's assume that you do the same.

Take the deck from the card case and give the cards a riffle shuffle, keeping the ace of spades on top and the ace of clubs on the bottom. This is quite easy to do, as you'll see when you give it a try.

Set the deck on the table. If you hand it to a spectator at this point, he just might idly shuffle the cards, which would ruin the trick.

Ambrose is good at following instructions, so enlist his aid.

Say, "Ambrose, I'd like you to think of any number from one to ten. Do you have a number? Good. Now, please change your mind and choose another number. I want to make sure everyone knows that this is not a psychological stunt."

Once Ambrose has his number, continue: "Now please think of a suit—clubs, hearts, spades, or diamonds. Put that together in your mind and you are thinking of a specific playing card. By the way, if you thought of the number one, that would be an ace, of course. Next, with your help, I'll try to divine the name of that card."

Turn your back and say, "Concentrate on the value of your card, please." After a moment, say, "I can't seem to get it.

Maybe we can make the thought waves more concrete. Would you pick up the deck and deal into a pile a number of cards equal to the value of the card you thought of. For instance, if you thought of the number eight, please deal eight cards into a pile. But deal very quietly so that I won't hear how many you're dealing."

Chat for a moment of the difficulties you're encountering. Then continue: "I'm still not getting it, Ambrose. Let's try something else; we'll get back to the value. Concentrate on the color of the card you chose, Ambrose. Think red . . . or black." Pause. "It's not clear. Do me a favor. If the card is red, very quietly deal one card onto your pile. If not, don't deal anything."

A brief pause.

"I'm not getting it. Back to the value. Ambrose, again would you deal a number equal to the value of your card onto your pile."

Once more, you complain bitterly of the tremendous task you've undertaken. "Gosh! I just *can't* get the value. Let's try the suits again. Ambrose, if the card you're thinking of is a spade or diamond, please quietly deal *two* cards onto the pile. Otherwise, do nothing." Pause.

"I can't understand it. Nothing seems to work. Maybe if I actually see the faces of the cards, I can figure it out. Ambrose, place the rest of the cards you're holding on top of the cards you've dealt off. Even all the cards up."

At this point, you turn back to the group; you want to make sure that Ambrose gives the deck a proper cut when you provide the next instruction.

"Please give the deck a complete cut. And you can give the cards another cut if you wish." Since a complete cut doesn't destroy the basic order of the cards, he can cut them any number of times.

Take the deck from Ambrose and hold it so that you are

looking at the face of the bottom card. Begin fanning through the cards. "Maybe if I see your card, I'll know it."

You are looking for the ace of spades, the first card Ambrose dealt off. When you get to the ace of spades, mentally count it as one. Continue counting the cards as you fan through the deck, until you get to the ace of clubs. Count the card *before* the ace of clubs, but do not count the ace of clubs. (While fanning through the deck, it is more efficient—and less obvious that you are counting—if you count by threes.) The number of cards you counted is the same number as Ambrose counted into his pile. This is your *key number*. You must remember this number; it not only will tell you the value of the chosen card, but also the suit.

Here's what you do to determine the value of the thought-of card: Divide the key number by two. (*Disregard the remainder.*) Either this will be the value of the card, or the card will be the next lower value. How can you tell which is correct? Easy. Just find out whether the chosen card is odd or even.

Suppose that the key number is 14. You divide this by 2, getting 7. Since seven is an odd number, you say, "Ambrose, I get a strong feeling that your card is an odd-numbered card, is that right?" If he says yes, you know that the value actually is seven. If he says no, you know that the value is the next lower number, six.

Suppose that the key number is 21. You divide this by two, getting 10. (There is a remainder of one, but you *always disregard the remainder.*) Since ten is an even number, you say, "Ambrose, I get a strong feeling that your card is an even-numbered card, is that right?" If he says yes, you know that the value actually is ten. If he says no, you know that the value is the next lower number, nine.

Incidentally, when you get a positive answer to your query, say, "I thought so." When you get a negative answer, say,

"So much for strong feelings. I'd better concentrate harder."

At this point in the performance, you should pause and mentally review your calculations to make sure you have the right value.

Once you have the value of the thought-of card, the rest is easy. For the suit, double the value of the chosen card and subtract that amount from the key number. (Say the value of the chosen card is 6 and the key number is 14. Double 6, giving you 12. Subtract 12 from 14, getting 2.) If the result is zero, the suit is clubs; if the result is one, the suit is hearts; if the result is two, the suit is spades; if the result is three, the suit is diamonds. This order is easily remembered by using this mnemonic:

CHaSeD—Clubs, Hearts, Spades, Diamonds
0 = Clubs, 1 = Hearts, 2 = Spades, 3 = Diamonds

Once you have figured out the suit and value, fan through the deck, remove the thought-of card, and place it face down onto the table. Ask Ambrose to name his card. Have him turn the tabled card face up.

Review
1) You have the ace of spades on top of the deck and the ace of clubs on the bottom.
2) Turn your back and have the spectator think of any number from one to ten. To this, he mentally adds a suit.
3) He deals a number equal to the value of his card into a pile.
4) Onto that same pile, he deals one card if his card is red and none if his card is black.
5) He again deals a number equal to the value of his card onto the pile.
6) He deals two cards onto the pile if his card is a spade or a diamond (the last two suits in the mnemonic CHaSeD).

7) He places the rest of the deck on top of the pile. Then he gives the deck as many complete cuts as he wishes.

8) Starting at the bottom of the deck, you fan through, looking at the faces of the cards. When you reach the ace of spades, you count it as one and continue counting until you reach the ace of clubs. You count the card before the ace of clubs, but not the ace itself. This is your key number.

9) Divide the key number by two. (*Disregard the remainder.*) The thought-of card is either this number or the next lower number.

10) If the result of dividing the key number by two is an odd number, say that you think the thought-of card is odd. If the spectator agrees, your number is correct; if he denies this, the selection is the next lower number. If the result of dividing the key number by two is an even number, say that you think the card is even. If the spectator agrees, your number is correct; if he denies it, the selection is the next lower number.

11) Double the value of the chosen card and subtract that amount from the key number. The result tells you the suit:

$$0 = \text{Clubs}$$
$$1 = \text{Hearts}$$
$$2 = \text{Spades}$$
$$3 = \text{Diamonds}$$

AN OLD-TIMER

Here's a trick so old that it has long since been forgotten by most older magicians and is unknown to younger ones. In its original form, it was colorful and effective. I have revitalized the trick, providing an improved handling and a new climax. Also, there is a one-in-five chance of performing a miracle.

Ask Paul to shuffle the deck. Take the cards back, saying, "I'm going to deal out some cards, forming a mystical pattern." You deal the cards face up like this:

```
           1              2

    3      4      5      6      7

           8              9

   10     11     12     13     14

          15             16
```

"Paul, you'll notice that there are four rows of five cards each."

(Actually, there are two rows and two columns, but the spectators generally don't care about this distinction.) You indicate each of the rows by running your hand across or down it (Illus. 110).

"Please think of any one of these cards." Avert your head as he does so.

"Now, with my mysterious, mystical, magical powers, I'll identify the very card you thought of." Stare briefly into Paul's eyes. Study the cards carefully. Another stare into Paul's eyes. "But it might take me a little while. I'm just not getting it."

At last, an inspiration: "Paul, your card could be in one of four rows or it could be all by itself. Wherever it is, would you please pick up a row which contains your card." He picks up one of the rows. (He can pick up the cards in any order.)

After Paul has picked up his row, only one other five-card row remains. You pick that one up.

"Please mix up your cards, like this." Give the cards you picked up a quick overhand shuffle.

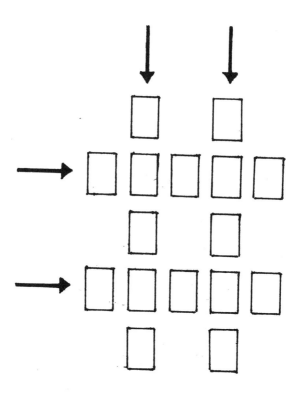

ILLUS. 110

After Paul mixes his five cards, take them from him and place them face down on top of the face-down pile you're holding.

Pick up the remaining six cards that are on the table and put them face down on top of all.

"Here, I'll give them a little extra mixing." You now perform my "One–Two–Three Shift," explained in detail starting on page 22. In this instance, you transfer 11 cards from the top of the pile to the bottom.

Drop the packet on top of the deck, saying, "Maybe we should try an even more mystical pattern."

Pick up the deck and deal 11 cards face up in this order:

1	2		3	4
		5		
6	7		8	9
10				11

You deal the next four cards so that each one lands in one of the positions marked with an X. It doesn't matter which one goes where.

X				X
1	2	X	3	4
		5		
6	7	X	8	9
10				11

Any X could be the chosen card. Also, the top card of the deck could be the chosen card. "Notice that in this formation, there are four rows with five cards in each row." As before, indicate each row by running your hand along it. Two of the rows are diagonal and two are horizontal (Illus. 111).

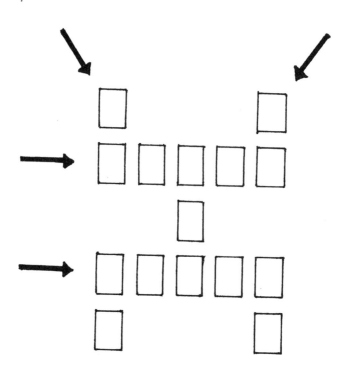

Again, stare into Paul's eyes and then study the cards. "No good," you declare at length. "What row is your card in?" As soon as he indicates a row, you know the chosen card, for it's the only X card in that row. A good conclusion is to pass your hand over the row slowly, back and forth, finally letting it fall onto the chosen card. "Is this it?" you ask. Naturally.

Suppose, however, that you ask which row the card is in, and Paul looks puzzled, finally telling you that his card isn't there. "Of course not," you say. "It's right here." Flip the top card of the deck face up.

As you can see, this superior ending will occur, on the average, once every five times.

The Name Doesn't Matter

Arun Bonerjee came up with an excellent trick based on a principle that is fairly well known among magicians. Wally Wilson showed me his version, in which he added a few subtle touches. I also added a touch or two.

Since Ginger really pays attention, she is the perfect choice to be your assistant. Hand her the deck and ask her to give it a shuffle.

"Now please deal the cards into a pile on the table."

She might ask, "How many?" or, "All of them?"

You say, "It doesn't matter."

But, of course, it *does* matter, at least to you. As she deals the cards, you apparently pay no attention, but actually count them.

She may deal only a small number of cards. When this happens, say, "Go ahead. We should have a fairly substantial pile."

After Ginger has dealt 13 or so, say, "Stop whenever you wish."

In any instance, make sure you know the number she finally deals. Let's say the number is 17.

You turn your back.

"I'd like you to mentally picture a pair of dice. In your mind, please select one of those dice. Roll that die and look at the number on top. But don't choose that number. Roll that die again. Do you see the number on top?

"Good. That's your number." Clearly, you're asking her to choose a number from one to six, but this method enhances the trick and sets the tone for the superb mental climax.

"Ginger, please quietly count that number of cards from your packet and hide them somewhere. Put them in your pocket or under something so that I won't be able to see them.

"Now please take a look at the card that lies at that number from the top of your packet. Remember that card and leave it at that position in the packet. In other words, if you hid three cards, you'd look at the third card from the top of the packet."

When she's done, turn back to the group.

"Ginger, if this is going to work, we'll require the strength of at least two people—you and one other person. So would you please think of the first name of someone you admire. What is that name?"

She tells you. Let's suppose the name is Ralph. "Please spell out that name, moving one card from the top to the bottom of your pile for each letter."

If you haven't already figured out the number of letters in the name, count them to yourself as she moves the cards from the top to the bottom of the pile. In this instance, you count five cards for R–A–L–P–H.

You now have two numbers in mind: the number she dealt off originally—in this example, 17; and the number in the name she spelled—in this case, five.

Subtract the number of cards in the name (5) from the total she dealt off at the beginning (17). Seventeen minus 5 gives you 12. This is the number of cards you must move from the top to the bottom of the packet.

"I'll mix the cards a bit."

You now perform my "One–Two–Three Shift," explained in detail starting on page 22, transferring 12 cards from the top to the bottom of the packet. This brings the chosen card to the bottom of the packet. (I know that this doesn't seem likely, but it nonetheless works.)

In some sneaky way, you must now peek at that bottom card. Here are three possibilities; choose whichever one seems most natural to you:

1) After you mix the cards, briefly tap them onto the table on their long sides to even them up. The backs are toward the spectators, and the faces are toward you. Thus, you can easily catch a glimpse of the bottom card. Hand the packet to Ginger and ask her to give them an additional shuffle.

2) Ask Ginger to give the cards a shuffle. Grip the packet at the rear end with your right hand, fingers on top and thumb on the bottom. As you hand the packet to Ginger, tip it forward ever so slightly so that you can get a peek at the bottom card (Illus. 112).

3) Turn slightly to the right as you comment, "You know, Ginger, you really ought to shuffle the cards too." You're holding the cards in your left hand in the position preceding an over-hand shuffle. Let the cards tilt a bit toward the group (Illus. 113). Glance down, taking a quick look at the bottom card, as you take the cards in your right hand and perform a brief overhand shuffle. (It's perfectly natural that you should take a look at your hands as you begin the shuffle.) Immediately hand the packet to Ginger for her to mix the cards.

ILLUS. 112   ILLUS. 113

As Ginger shuffles the cards, provide this review: "I had no way of knowing what number you'd think of, nor could I know what name you'd come up with. So if I go through the packet and find your card, would that be a good trick?"

The correct answer is yes. "Well, I don't want to do a trick. Instead, I'd like to try to read your mind. Fan the cards out, faces toward you, please. Now place your finger on your chosen card and concentrate on it."

Pause. "And, wherever you are, Ralph, please help her concentrate." After a suitable pause, you gradually reveal the card—first naming the color, then the suit, and finally the value.

Note

As you no doubt have discerned, the whole business of having her think of a name and spell it out is nothing more than a smoke screen.

A KINGLY DECISION

Joe Hustler invented this extraordinarily effective trick. You must perform it to see what a strong result you get with a minimum amount of labor. A modest amount of preparation is necessary.

Remove from the deck the four kings. Place the king of clubs on top. The other three kings should be placed near the bottom. I generally put one on the bottom, one third from the bottom, and one fifth from the bottom.

Darla is excellent at shuffling the cards, so you should solicit her help. But first, you have some shuffling of your own to do. Give the deck two good riffle shuffles.

Hand the deck to Darla, saying, "Please give the cards a little over-hand shuffle."

Once she takes the deck, pantomime the over-hand shuffling motion. She should give the deck *only one* over-hand shuffle. If she looks as though she might continue shuffling, place your hand on top of her hands and say, "I want you to listen carefully." This effectively stops her from giving the cards the extra shuffle that will spoil the trick.

Turn away from the group. "Darla, hold the deck so that the faces are toward you and no one else can see the faces of any of the cards. Now fan through and take out the first king that you come to. Hide that card somewhere. You can put it into a pocket, sit on it, whatever."

The first king that she comes to is the king of clubs.

"Next, take out the king that's the same color as the one you took. Please put that king in Herb's pocket." Obviously, you name one of the males who is present.

Turn back and face the group. Concentrate fiercely. At length point at Herb and declare, "The card in your pocket, Herb, is the king of spades. And, of course, Darla's king is the king of clubs."

TRIPLE TELEPATHY

Stewart Judah came up with the original trick. It is little known and its climax is absolutely astounding. I have changed the handling slightly.

A modest amount of memory work is required. You must remember the number of cards that a spectator deals, and, later, you must also remember the name of a specific card. Not too tough, actually.

Let's assume that three ladies agree to cooperate in an experiment in telepathy.

Ask Sarah to shuffle the deck. Take it back and silently count off 15 cards from the top. Count the cards by three so that it will not be obvious that you're counting them.

Hand the 15 cards to Sarah, saying, "Please shuffle these. Then deal as many of them as you wish into a pile. Look at the last card you deal into the pile and remember it. Put it back and place the rest of your cards on top of it."

Make sure your directions are understood.

The next few seconds are extremely critical. You must seem totally uninterested in what Sarah is doing. Actually, you're counting the number of cards that she deals into a pile. *Remember* that number. Say it over to yourself several times till the end of the trick.

To cover the fact that you're counting the number of cards being dealt, you might act slightly befuddled, saying something like, "Let's see. Now who was our next volunteer?"

Point to the pile on the table, and address Beth: "So far, we have one chosen card in the middle of a shuffled pile. Now, I'd appreciate it if you'd cut off a pile from the deck."

Hold out the remaining cards. After she cuts off a pile, continue, "Shuffle those and look at your bottom card. That will be your chosen card." As you say, "Shuffle those . . . ," do so with the cards you're holding. When you add, ". . . look at your bottom card," slightly tip the cards you're holding and take a casual glance at the bottom card. Remember this card; it's your *key card.* As Beth continues following your directions, give your packet another over-hand shuffle. Make sure you shuffle off the last few cards individually so that the bottom card, which you know, becomes the top card.

You are now remembering the number of cards that Sarah dealt into a pile and the name of the top card of the packet you're holding—your key card.

Ask Beth to place her packet onto the table.

Approach Louise, fanning the cards from hand to hand.

"Please take any one of these cards." After she selects a card, close up the cards and place them in a face-down pile onto the table. "Please look at your card and then place it on top of the pile." Point to the pile you just set onto the table.

Time to toss a bit of stardust into the eyes of all.

Point to the first pile, saying, "Now we have a card in the middle . . ." Point to the second pile. ". . . and a card on the bottom . . ." Point to the third pile. ". . . and a card on top. And all the piles have been shuffled. So let's lose that last card by placing *this* pile on top of it." Indicate that Sarah should place her pile on top of Louise's pile. Turn to Beth. "And let's lose your card by placing your pile on top of all." Indicate that Beth should place her pile on top of the combined piles. Each spectator gives the deck one complete cut. "The deck is thoroughly mixed. Since there's no way I could know any one of the selected cards, I must try telepathy."

Ask Louise to concentrate. Fan through the cards, faces toward yourself, studying them carefully. Cut the key card to the top (or back) of the deck. The card that is facing you belongs to Louise. Tentatively take it and place it face down in front of Louise.

Turn to Sarah. "Please concentrate on your card also." Now you must recall the number that Sarah dealt off at the beginning. Starting with the card that is now on the bottom, count that many. The card at that number from the bottom is Sarah's card. Ponder a bit, finally placing the card face down in front of Sarah.

Now it's Beth's turn to concentrate. Continue counting from the previous number until you reach 15. The next card will be Beth's. Place it face down in front of her.

Each spectator in turn names her card and turns it over.

Review

1) Sarah shuffles the deck and gives it back. You subtly count off 15 cards from the top of the deck and hand these to her, telling her to shuffle them, deal some into a pile, and then look at and remember the last card she deals. She replaces this card on the dealt-off pile and puts the remainder of the 15 cards on top.

2) You seem to be paying no attention, but you actually count the number Sarah deals off. You must remember that number.

3) Hold out the remainder of the deck to Beth, asking her to cut off a pile. She shuffles these and then looks at and remembers the bottom card.

4) As you demonstrate how Beth is to shuffle her cards, you sneak a peek at the bottom card of those remaining in your hand. With an over-hand shuffle, you move this card to the

top of the packet. You are now remembering two things: the number of cards counted off by Sarah and the name of the card on top of the packet you're holding—your key card.

5) Tell Beth to place her packet onto the table.

6) Fan the cards you're holding from hand to hand, asking Louise to choose one. After she does, you close up the packet and place it face down onto the table. Louise looks at her card and then places it on top of the packet you just set onto the table.

7) Have Sarah put her pile on top of Louise's pile. Have Beth put her pile on top of all.

8) Each spectator gives the deck one complete cut.

9) Fan through the cards, faces toward yourself. Cut the key card to the top (or back) of the deck. The card facing you is Louise's. Place it face down in front of her.

10) Recall the number that Sarah dealt off. Starting with the card that is now at the face of the deck, count that many. The card at that number from the face of the deck is Sarah's card. Place it face down in front of her.

11) Continue counting from the previous number until you reach 15. The next card is Beth's. Place it face down in front of her.

12) Each spectator in turn names her card and then turns it over.

BEHIND THE BACK

Ronald J. Dayton came up with this very subtle idea: You look over the group carefully and then choose as your assistant Ralph, whom you know to be a good sport.

"Ralph, we're going to test your telepathic ability. Please turn away from the group for a moment."

While Ralph's back is turned, fan the deck out face up and have Gloria touch one of the cards. Close up the deck and tell Ralph that he can rejoin the group. In fact, you maneuver

Ralph so that he's at the front of the group. You and he are facing everyone else.

"Ralph, I'm going to have you look right at the person who selected a card. As you do so, concentrate and see if the name of the card comes to you.

"The entire card may come to you in a flash. Or the card could come to you as a number and the initial of the suit. The 6 of clubs, for instance, could come to you as 6C." Maneuver Ralph so he's directly facing Gloria.

"Are you getting the name of the card, Ralph?" He is. What's more, he names the selected card.

You can repeat the stunt a time or two. Ralph might not get each selection perfectly, but he demonstrates absolutely that he has telepathic powers.

Is Ralph a confederate? Not to begin with. In fact, you could choose anyone who's a good sport.

As you maneuver Ralph around to face Gloria, you keep your right hand behind his back. After you explain how the card might come to him as a number and a digit, you *trace the name of the card on his back with your first finger.* If the selection were the 8 of spades, you would trace *8S* on his back. If it were the queen of hearts, you would trace *QH*.

Ralph might not interpret your tracing perfectly, but he should get enough of it to demonstrate his amazing powers.

Note

For guaranteed results, you can work with someone you know and do some practice ahead of time.

No Sleight Trick

This trick originally called for considerable sleight of hand. I've eliminated this and added several possible conclusions.

Howard always seems quite suggestible, so he'd be perfect for this trick. Hand him the deck of cards and ask him to shuffle it.

"Now, Howard, please cut the deck into three fairly equal piles." Make sure the piles are nearly the same. If there is a disparity, you might say, "That's equal?"

When you're satisfied with the piles, say, "Howard, pick up any one of the piles, take a card from it, and show it around."

After he does so, say, "Set your pile back down onto the table and put your card on top of it." He does. "Even up your pile, cut it in the middle, and complete your cut." If Howard is as suggestible as you think, he should cut the pile quite close to the middle.

"Now set your pile on top of one of the others, and then place the last pile on top."

Howard's card is now quite close to the middle of the deck.

You take the deck and, cutting it as close as you can to the middle, riffle-shuffle the two halves together. As you take the two halves, preliminary to the shuffle you should be able to get a good look at the bottom card of one of the halves. Remember this card; it's your *key card*. And when you riffle-shuffle, make sure that this becomes the bottom card of the deck.

Invite Howard to give the deck a complete cut. Actually, the deck can be given any number of complete cuts. Spread the deck face up onto the table, fanning the cards out so that all can be seen.

"Howard, I'd like you to pick out five cards from various parts of the deck. And make one of them the card you chose. I'm going to watch closely, so be as sneaky as you can. It won't matter, really, because I'm certain I'll be able to read your mind."

As Howard starts to remove the cards, note where your key card is. His chosen card will either be the key card, or it will be very close to it. So if he takes one card from near the key card and four others from other spots in the deck, you're all set.

Take the five cards from Howard and place them in a face-up row on the table. Pass your hand over them until some mysterious force causes you to drop your hand on top of one card.

"I feel that this is your card, Howard."

All are dumbfounded.

They will probably be equally astounded if you use this conclusion: Howard is holding the five cards face up. You note at what position the chosen card lies. Ask him to turn the pile face down. If his chosen card is now second from the top, all is well. Otherwise, you must bring it to that position.

Suppose it's at the bottom of the pile. Say, "As you know, Howard, three is a mystic number. Please deal three cards into a pile. Now place the rest of your cards on top." His chosen card is now second from the top.

What if the chosen card is at the top of the pile? Have him deal off three cards, drop the rest on top, and then repeat the process. Again, the chosen card is second from the top.

If the chosen card is fourth from the top, have him turn his pile face up. The chosen card is now second from the top of the face-up pile.

If the chosen card is third, the procedure is slightly different, as I'll explain in a moment.

His chosen card is now second from the top of the group of five. You direct Howard through a down-under deal. "Please deal a card onto the table, and place the next card on the bottom of your packet. Deal another one onto the table, and put the next card on the bottom." He continues until he's holding only one card. It's the one he chose.

If Howard's card is third from the top, you have him perform an under-down deal. The first card goes under the packet, the next one goes onto the table, and so on. Again, he ends up with his selected card.

Note

When Howard picks out his five cards, he might just take two from fairly close to your key card. Clearly, the chosen card could be either one of these. When you take the five cards from him, arrange it so that these are the top two.

Study the faces of the cards. Note and remember the top card. "I can't seem to figure it out. I want these out of my sight while I concentrate." Stick the five cards into your pocket. After trancing for several seconds, remove four cards from your pocket, leaving the top one there.

Do not spread out the cards.

Hold the four cards in the dealing position in your left hand. Bring your right hand to the deck, ready to deal. "I believe I have your card, Howard. What is it?" There are two possibilities:

1) If he does not name the card in your pocket, you know that it must be the top card of the packet. Deal it off the top of the packet, turning it over. "And there it is!" Return the rest of the packet to your pocket, adding the pocketed card to the bottom. "You know what the key is, don't you?" Pat your pocket. "Getting the cards out of sight." Bring out the four cards and add them to the deck. Put the chosen card face down on top of the deck as well.

2) If Howard names the card in your pocket, immediately turn over the top card of the packet, saying, "That's not it." Drop the card face up onto the table. Continue in the same way with the other three cards. "I believe I have it . . ." Pull the chosen card from your pocket and show it. ". . . right here!"

THE FORCE IS WITH YOU

The brilliant Wally Wilson recently developed a wonderful force that works particularly well as a mental trick. I'm grateful that he recommended it for this book.

Ask Stan to give the deck a shuffle. Take the cards back and say, "Stan, I could fan out the cards face up and ask you to think of a card, but you might feel that one card is more significant than the others. In other words, you might make a psychological choice." As you talk, hold the cards face up so that all can see the faces. Fan off a group of ten cards or so, saying, "You might think of one of these, for instance."

Place the group at the rear of the deck (on top if the deck were face down). Make sure you note the last card you fanned to, which is now the rearmost card (the top card if the deck were face down). You must remember this card. What's more, it must not be an obvious card, which the spectator might remember. The best choice would be a spot card. Let's say that the card you're remembering is the 6 of clubs.

You have just placed a packet to the rear of the face-up deck. "Or you might think of one of these . . ." Fan out five cards and place them at the rear of the deck, just as you did the previous group. ". . . or one of these . . ." Fan out five more cards and place them at the rear. ". . . or one of these." Fan out a significant number of cards, lift them off the deck, and then replace them onto the face-up deck. Close up the deck and turn it face down. Say: "So you could look through the deck and think of a card, but some cards might stand out. In fact, you may have seen a card that stood out from the others. Let's avoid that."

Hand Stan the deck. "Instead, I'd like you to think of a number . . . say, from one to ten. Got one? Okay, now please change your mind. Again, we want to make sure you don't make a psychological choice." Pause. "I'll turn away, and I'd like you to deal that many cards onto the table . . . very quietly. Now hide them somewhere; put them into your pocket or stick them under something."

When Stan finishes, turn back and take the balance of the deck. Count off ten cards from the top of the deck, taking them one *under* the other. In other words, the cards should retain their order.

Turn the packet face up. "Stan, I'm going to go through these cards. Please remember the card that lies at the number you thought of." (The card at that number will be the card you're remembering—in our example, the 6 of clubs.)

"Here, I'll deal them into your hand." He holds one of his

hands out, palm up. Make it very obvious that you're averting your head, so that you can't see the cards as you deal. Slowly deal the face-up pile one card at a time onto Stan's palm, counting aloud as you do so.

When you're done, take the cards from Stan and place them face down on top of the deck. Have Stan cut the deck.

Hold the deck to your forehead and gradually reveal the name of the card: "I see clouds, dark clouds. Your card is black . . . I'd say it's a club. Think of the value. I'm starting to get it . . . Yes, it's rounded . . . maybe a 9. No, no . . . *like* a 9 . . . It's a 6. Your card is the 6 of clubs."

INDEX